THE BACKYARD
Lumberjack

THE BACKYARD
Lumberjack

The ULTIMATE GUIDE to **FELLING, BUCKING, SPLITTING & STACKING**

Frank Philbrick & Stephen Philbrick

Storey Publishing

The mission of Storey Publishing is to serve our customers by publishing practical information that encourages personal independence in harmony with the environment.

Edited by Deborah Balmuth and Carleen Madigan Perkins
Cover design by Kent Lew
Interior design and layout by Vicky Vaughn
Cover photographs © Adam Mastoon
Interior photography credits found on page 160
Color illustrations by Dan Thompson. Additional illustrations by Gregory Wenzel, except on page 120 © Elayne Sears.
Indexed by Christine R. Lindemer, Boston Road Communications

Printed in Hong Kong by Elegance
10 9 8 7 6 5 4 3 2 1

LIBRARY OF CONGRESS CATALOGING-IN-PUBLICATION DATA

Philbrick, Frank.
  The backyard lumberjack : the ultimate guide to felling, bucking, splitting & stacking / Frank Philbrick
    and Stephen Philbrick.
      p. cm.
  Includes bibliographical references and index.
  ISBN-13: 978-1-58017-634-7; ISBN-10: 1-58017-634-8 (pbk. : alk. paper)
  ISBN-13: 978-1-58017-651-4; ISBN-10: 1-58017-651-8 (hardcover : alk. paper)
  1. Tree felling. 2. Woodlots. 3. Fuelwood.
  I. Philbrick, Stephen.
  II. Title.

SD538.P49 2006
634.9'8—dc22

                                                                              2006015207

To Deb, for coming across the road; Ma and KT, for the
patience and support; and B&C, without whom . . .
—F.P.

To cold winters,
hot stoves,
stout maple,
spry sons
—S.P.

CONTENTS

THOREAU ONCE NOTED that firewood warms you twice, once when you split it and once when you burn it. If you still feel that way after felling your own trees, bucking them up, and then splitting and stacking all the wood, write me and I'll pull my copy of *Walden* out of the ash heap. This is a process that can warm

and fortify your body and soul a hundred times over. It is also a connection to our past and to skills and strengths most people never discover or use. Think of the intimacy early settlers must have had with their axes, adzes, bucksaws, and mauls. Everyone on the frontier must have been able to handle these items as adroitly as today's lumberjacks do their chain saws. The clearing of land was the culture, and the ax its first ambassador.

The woods we have spent our time in are of three basic types, each common to New England: upland hardwood forests, upland evergreen-dominated forests, and swampy areas (from the last, we expended a fair amount of time snaking what hardwoods we could). Good burning wood is much scarcer in the latter two environs, and there is more work to get it out. Red and swamp maples are the main quarry in the wet conditions; ash, beech, yellow and white birch, maple, and cherry grow well in sections side by side with hemlock and white pine on our hilltop.

We would not have spent thousands of hours in the woods if we hadn't enjoyed them. More than that, they allowed us, both together and separately, to think and speak in an uncommonly free and honest manner. To this I would add that we have each observed things in nature that one would not normally associate with the keening snarl of a chain saw. My brother Charlie ("Tood" from here on out; don't ask) and my father still speak of the paper wasp they saw laying eggs in the end grain of some maple. The delicate, corset-waisted, bottle-blue creature positioned itself like a well-drilling rig and inserted an impossibly long, flimsy needle right into what must have been some sort of microtubule in the sapwood. Whatever it was that hatched, they saw its genesis.

One evening that could have been any stark fall evening, Dad got an odd feeling in his gut and turned to face a black bear for a long moment. After looking at the noisy intruder, the bear eventually turned and took up its activities where it had left off. Dad returned to his civilized mind from the animal place such a sight had sent him.

I was once stopped short by the stunning, blissful forensics of a late-night murder, or meal, depending on your allegiance. Knee-deep in snow on the way to the woodlot I saw the businesslike progress of a chipmunk's tracks. As they were going my way, I paid some attention. Soon enough the spacing of the tracks shortened up and then described an abrupt buttonhook. Not three steps back the way he'd come there were twin angel wings in the snow. Two long, serrated crescents enfolded the delicate tracks and no more. Actually seeing and understanding the evidence of such an encounter warmed a visceral but deductive part of me. The silent, incontrovertible evidence of an owl's dimly foreseen attack chilled me in just the opposite way. Everyone has had that same moment in which he or she glimpsed, but radically underestimated, impending tragedy. Gaining confirmation that this sickening moment has its roots threaded honestly in the natural world was reassuring to someone afraid of having all animal influence bleached out by civilization.

During the fall we spent writing this book, Dad got ill, first with pneumonia, then bronchitis, then stubborntosis, and finally back to pneumonia. Tood had been talking to Dad on the horn and worrying that he was going to make things even worse for himself by trying to work right through his illness. We decided that we both had to go home and get the firewood in. I knew how hard it was for Dad to need help; in fact, I was sure it was the hard-est part of the illness. Tood and I hadn't had the chance to spend real time together in a long while, and in retrospect, we may never be living under the same roof again. Everyone was looking forward to the time together for different reasons.

The year before, Dad had felled the two dozen trees we would need, so it remained to snake them out of the woods, buck them up, split them, and stack them. Over the course of two and a half days, Tood and I ran saws and split with mauls almost nonstop. Both of us have gone through long periods of our lives with calluses lining our hands, but we had each softened up considerably in the months preceding this unexpected trial. By the end of the third day I had sweat out every beer I'd bought in the city, and Tood had torn rows of neat ovals off both hands. The memory of the fingers is fiercely loyal, but very short-term.

The splitting and stacking done, we drank some beer and caught up on stillness. Dad was sorry he couldn't have helped more, he said. If you had, we wouldn't have gotten this chance, we said. I thought about how I've never come across an activity so conducive to easy talking, a perfect pastime both mindless and skilled with which to use up some time. Some time in the fall and some in the winter getting ready for next year. Look in your woods or dooryard. There's room for this.

ALTHOUGH I WASN'T BORN INTO IT —
splitting wood, that is — the first time I tried
it I knew I was born *for* it. The constructive
destruction involved in felling, bucking, and
splitting was a deep thrill, a coming-home
feeling that hasn't changed over the past
33 years.

I come from a poetic and academic family and have pursued the writing part of my heritage. My kids and I grew up in Cummington, Massachusetts, where we raised sheep; heated with wood; made lots of hay and a little maple syrup; played and coached baseball; had adventures in the woods; went to school (mostly the kids); drove a bus; and worked at the general store. Apparently inevitably, I became the minister of the West Cummington Congregational Church 10 years ago. I love it. The family is bearing up pretty well. I am as at home now in the pulpit as I am in the woods, although I dress better for the latter occupation (those red suspenders . . .).

During my time in the woodlot and by the woodpile I have done a bit of figuring. Frank and I have calculated (very roughly) that we leave a quarter to a third of a cord of firewood on the forest floor every year in the form of sawdust. Oh well, it's mulch, it's compost; it's as much the future as the past.

Another triumph was the end-to-end puzzle. Laid end-to-end, how far would our year's supply of firewood reach? Before we began figuring, we made predictions. Are these predictions guesses about the fact or the figuring? No matter. The estimates, I believe, were "from here to the store" and "from here to Nebraska." Well, at 900 sticks of stove wood per cord ("Wait a minute. Pieces as we cut 'em or after we split 'em?" "How about, as they go into the stove?' "Then they'd be burned up." "After we split 'em, then." "OK."). As I was saying, at 900 pieces of wood per cord, and 12 cords per year for the house and the pottery studio, we estimated nearly 11,000 pieces of firewood. If each one were 18 inches long, let's see, they would stretch 16,500 feet. That's about 3 miles; only halfway to the store. ("Well, in our lifetimes do you think we'd reach Nebraska? How about the state line?")

One of the thrills of felling trees is the power and the sheer decibels of the chain saw, especially for those of us who don't play electric guitar. When the saw is turned off and the rest of the world comes back, it is a delight to have someone to share that world and the work with. Much of our relationship has been produced by work. Much work has been produced by our relationship. Some of the work created has been for therapists, including physical, but most of it has been ours, in the woods and at the woodpile.

The hard work with a loud and dangerous saw is a current flowing from one island of conversation, one season, one age to the next. The figuring was a rehearsal for the passing of time; and for passing. The boy who began work with me as soon as he could walk always gloried in what he could do now: carry a full bucket of grain, then a bucket of water, then a bucket of water in each hand. And he always pushed up hard against what he couldn't do. As we worked, I noticed (and gloried in) each little change. Until one day it dawned on me that my son was a man — and had been for quite some time. The year I had pneumonia brought it home. It was September and I couldn't get the firewood in. Frank and Charlie (the truly laid-back lumberjack) came back and in a week had 10 cords cut and split in a huge mound in the backyard. I don't know who was more proud.

What we have left unsaid is all that we wanted to hear from each other — and there has been enough quiet and enough laughter in the woods for most of it to dare to creep out.

I have watched woodpiles increase and dwindle as we have all grown up. In anger, I have split wood instead of skulls. I have sometimes retreated into the woods in order to become a better member of my community. All the physics and engineering I know I have learned by dropping trees. My joyful noise has come out of a chain saw and the sound of a good clean hit, the cry of "Timber!" and the depths of my heart.

I have fed hundreds of cords of innocent wood into stoves and sap evaporators. Before I fell a tree, I offer my gratitude. Somehow the process of growth keeps on keeping ahead of us.

One year I decided to earn some real cash selling cordwood, even though I was equipped with only a chain saw, a maul, and a pickup. I cut, split, and delivered 31 cords. As my neighbor observed, I lost about $10 on each cord, but "made up for it in volume." Here's where I'm heading (all these stories have a point). When I told one of my sugaring partners about the whole enterprise, he asked,

"Seriously? You split 31 cords of wood by hand?"

"Yes."

"Man, you really are a poet!"

I've often wondered, did he mean "what an imagination?" or "what an idiot?" I admire that remark: a nice clean split leaving two halves of equal weight. Choose the one you want.

Stephen Millarich

Ten Reasons to Be a Backyard Lumberjack

THIS BOOK IS INTENDED FOR ANYONE who has the regional resources, the physical wherewithal, and most important, the desire to take down trees. You may find yourself in almost any climate and almost any population density. Dad used his first woodstove in a trailer in Georgia. I've seen woodpiles resting against mansions in Greenwich, Connecticut, and huge piles being stacked day by day alongside tarpaper shacks in the Northeast Kingdom of Vermont. My best friend through college cut his teeth splitting wood in suburban Michigan.

In our own backyard, in New England, we fell trees for firewood. Depending on your situation, though, you may have other motives.

1 The Woodsman's Workout

With the possible exception of its summertime counterpart, haying, I have never found a more diverse, engaging, adaptable, and productive workout than getting in wood for the winter. This is not a workout to embark upon if you don't keep yourself strong the rest of the year. There is significant torque, jarring motion, and repeated bending and lifting. Once the first few sessions are out of the way, though, you will find that your body falls into a rhythm, and it actually uses certain movements to help stretch and even to recover from motions that stress opposing sets of muscles. When you're really whaling along, you'll reach a point where the words "let's take a rest and split and stack" begin to sound like the advice of a wise woodsman. At this point you are probably not far from one of the following: a heart attack, nightfall, the emergency room, madness, or a cold beer.

2 A Sunny Yard

Could be that overhanging branches or tightly grouped trees are throwing too much shade on a garden plot, or threatening to come down on your house or garage in a storm. Unless the tilt of a nearby tree is extreme, you can learn to safely fell it away from buildings and, eventually, into your stove or wallet.

3 A Fatter Wallet

Tree services are quite expensive, but not for no reason. Trees that are likely to fall on buildings have to be climbed and felled 8 feet at a time, using expensive little saws and a variety of high-quality climbing equipment. The companies have to carry enormous insurance policies as well. Hiring these fine folks is not always necessary by any means, though, and you can learn whether a tree is safe to fell on your own.

4 Your Trees, Your Lumber

The option of taking wood from your property and using it is a real one. Dad had some locust cut into inch-thick slabs and built an outdoor staircase with them. This will last and last, because of naturally occurring preservatives in these trees. On a much larger scale, in terms of both volume produced and money spent, I once helped raise a timber-framed barn using only lumber harvested from a few hundred acres of nearby mixed hardwoods in the Berkshires.

5 Good Times on a Saturday Night

Most people are no longer connected by the work they do, or have done for them, in their homes. I think this is against our nature. I think

communities function better when work is shared. This would not be a hard change to effect in our world. Perhaps there is a neighbor or two you aren't still ducking about the lawn dwarf you accidentally shredded with the rented rototiller, and you and this friend could order wood together and spend a few weekends splitting it. There is something very easy about beginning an acquaintance through shared work.

 ## Awe-Filled Neighbors

People joke about lumberjacks as the epitome of manliness, but there is at least a little truth to the myth. In my travels and competition experience I've met some incredibly tough, quick, resilient men (and women), some of whom were lumberjacks only on the weekends and others who spent 50 hours a week dropping trees in the woods.

There is a toughness that eventually comes with enough exposure to working in the woods, with enough splinters and barked shins and mashed fingers. Anyone can build a tolerance to these things. With time, you'll also learn that so many little discomforts can just be ignored for the sake of a less stressful life (not to mention the rippling biceps; see Reason #1).

 ## A Grateful Town

It is admittedly rare that a chain saw can save the day, but occasionally a tree comes down and needs to be moved. Remember to stay calm and follow the simple rules and warnings we have learned by trial and mostly error. If you do, it could be *you* all over the thank-you board down at the town hall and not that snooty Mr. Jones with his winch that pulled Timmy out of the well.

8 Power Tools

If nothing else, you will discover the absolute adolescent joy of firing up a chain saw and laying waste to something. Maybe not laying waste, but how about methodically cutting a tree into straight and uniform sections? Hmm? Doesn't that sound wild and crazy? Okay, well, once I got bored with that and ran an old chain I didn't care to keep sharp all the way through a frozen couch. Stuffing and little chips of icy wafer-board were spitting everywhere, and I added at least five years to my life.

9 A Clear Head

Felling trees safely and turning them into firewood, bonfires, or building material can make you stronger and more confident and open your mind to the relaxation that can be had while working at a dynamic task. I remember splitting wood with a quiet lad who bottled his anger as a hobby. After he got warmed up and forgot the outside world, he hacked and flailed with a loosed energy I never expected. I didn't let him take the maul home, but I told him it was here anytime. I can readily imag-ine a successful therapy session punctuated by some violent, constructive work with a couple of 16-inch beech bolts. The maul could be tethered out of reach of the door (and the therapist's chair, for that matter). I might just build a convincing little faux shrink's office abutting our woodshed and get some work done while exorcising society's demons (and exercising them too). People have paid to do dumber stuff. (I didn't mean buying this book, of course, so read on.)

10 A Warm House

There is a temptation to see heating your house with wood as antiquated. It need not be, and I believe now is a good time to bring it back into our lives. At least in New England, there is more firewood to be responsibly cut than there has been since the end of the eighteenth century, and the price of fossil fuels is only going to climb in our future. Heating with wood also leads to a sense of spiritual purity and mental health that, I'll admit, is achievable through other methods. But you can't warm your house all winter with yoga mats. They don't even burn clean.

1 Into the WOODS

THERE ARE MANY REASONS WHY YOU might head for the woods with a chain saw, but one of the biggest for us (besides an obvious need to heat the house) is simply the desire to spend time in the forest. It's exciting to observe the woods and satisfying to interact with them, to become part of the local drama and ecology. Learning about the forest around us — how the trees grow, mature, and interact with each other — also helps us become better woodlot managers.

Our Backyard

If you gaze out your window right now, you are looking at a landscape affected by humans, in some cases in so many different times and ways that you may not be able to trace the various phases and uses of what you see. Here in New England, the landscape has been shaped over the centuries by forces ranging from selective burning by Native Americans to clear-cutting by nineteenth-century farmers to make way for sheep. During the decades between 1830 and 1880, New England suffered her most widespread deforestation, with 60 to 80 percent of the old growth clear-cut to make way for orchards, tillage, and grazing for sheep.

In the 1840s, the tariff on wool was lowered, and immediately sheep populations began to fall with the prices. This decline led to the rise of the white pine. Anyone who has ever driven through New England between late fall and early spring has doubtless observed odd, rectangular patches of evergreens on far-off hillsides. These are old fields filled with the first comers, and since white pines far outstrip hardwoods as saplings, any lapsed grazing grounds have gone to them. When walking at night it is tempting to imagine moonlit conversations filled with derision as stately rock maples, with their blood blued by aqua sugar tubing, sneer across tumbled stone walls at the nouveau pitch, crowded on the freshest real estate. Though these fields of white pine can still be seen throughout New England, many of them were harvested in the opening decades of the twentieth century. Seeing a valuable crop of second-growth trees, the timber industry leaped eagerly on these white pines for use as shipping crates.

Like a person holding a grudge, white pine is unable to resprout after being cut, and new hardwoods quickly took up the cause of their forebears, once again filling the fields. One of the characteristics of this generation of hardwoods is the multistemmed cluster of trees. Birch, black cherry, red maple, and red oak grow quickly in close groups and are now found abundantly on New England hillsides. For some linguistic reason lost in old works, there are a number of truly satisfying ways of referring to little clusters of trees like this; spinney, copse, coppice, thicket, and glen are but a few. To entertain yourself when nothing interesting is being said around a crudités tray or a saw-studded bedliner, try using them all in one sentence. The woods have a subtle, inexorable tendency away from the tidy borders we force on them, but every time I take a walk or look at a new woodlot, I can see where stone walls still delineate different species.

Managing Your Woods

The woods are not only a classroom but also a laboratory. The goal of woodlot management is to improve the quality of the timber left to grow and to provide firewood for next winter. We're assuming here that you're thinning a woodlot by practicing selective culling — that is, removing damaged trees, undesirable species, or trees that are growing too close to others. You should also remember that you can alter the habitat for wildlife — for better or worse — by culling or leaving certain species in your woodlot.

Let the light shine. This woodlot has trees of varying maturity, with enough space between them to let light reach the younger trees in the understory.

Managing a woodlot is not the same as grooming. Dead trees (hint: no leaves, slipping bark, fungi on trunk, woodpecker holes) can be good wood. Our usual rule is: If the trunk is still hard enough and has enough grain left to split, then it is worthwhile as firewood. When dead trees get "punky," they are already half burned (oxidized). They may look like a mess, but there is a virtue to leaving them alone. They aren't consuming resources. In fact, they *are* resources. That big old barkless monster, half rotten? Insects are having a harvest, and therefore woodpeckers are having a

A dense spot. These trees are all of a similar age and have grown so close together that very little sunlight can reach the forest floor.

A Word about Hilltowns

Our part of Massachusetts is called the Hilltowns, but, really, it could be compared to any number of places around the country, defined as much by the way people live as by a spot on the map. Some say the Hilltowns are a state of mind; others, a ridgy place between valleys. At the very least, it's a forested place where the rev of a chain saw is more common than the whine of a leafblower.

Today our Hilltowns are a strange mix of good ol' boys and nouveau country folk. Roads winding back through the hollows formed by tributaries to the rivers are just as likely punctuated by wrought-iron-sculpture mailboxes made by a hippy welder as they are to have Mallard decoy mailboxes set stoutly in concrete by the contractor/volunteer fireman who lives next door. "Next door" can refer to a house between 50 feet and 500 yards away.

Town meetings are punctuated by the usual ridiculous battles. There was once a row about manure falling on paved roads, and another concerning how often the church bell would ring. Small-town stuff mixed with the worries of the outside world.

field day. Seeing a pileated woodpecker is a real thrill; knowing that you are providing a habitat for these rare creatures is a quiet satisfaction. After that, the rotting tree is compost and enriches the soil for its upright neighbors. Remember, rotting and burning are both the process of oxidation at work. ("The slow smokeless burning of decay," as Robert Frost wrote in his poem "The Woodpile." When in doubt, Frost is usually as good a reference as anything else in the bookshelf. No Frost at home? Put this down and buy his complete poems instead.)

The tops and branches left after a timber harvest, called "slash," provide leaves and buds for deer to browse in the bitterest part of winter. So do the little-regarded hemlocks. The point is, humans think of some things as alive and some things as dead, but *all* of the forest is alive. Beech, bay, madrone, cherry, hackberry, shad, hornbeam, holly, black birch, maple, oak, walnut, butternut, chestnut, hickory, sweetgum, mulberry, pine, and fir are just some of the trees that feed birds and other woodland animals.

The woodlot will be more profitable and the environment healthier if you harvest the lumber trees. Left too long, they will shade out all competition. When they are finally cut,

Fungus is a sign. The presence of fungus on a tree is a sign of decay; this one is a good candidate to be felled for firewood.

What a punk. Trees that have decayed so much that the wood is "punky" shouldn't be used for firewood, because they've started to oxidize and won't throw much heat.

the remaining small, weak trees are overexposed to weather, both storms and sun. The Audubon Society, local foresters, and Cooperative Extension agents can all provide valuable information about how we influence bird and animal populations by our choices in tree populations.

As a rule of thumb, moderate thinning will yield one cord of firewood per acre per year. So, with a 5-acre woodlot you should be able to heat a well-insulated home year after year without depleting the woodlot. You can estimate the number of trees you'll need to cut by using the table in the appendix showing the relationship of tree diameter to cords of firewood (see page 153). A good rule for drafty old New England farmhouses, insulated by newspapers, mouse nests, and corncobs, is one cord of wood per room per winter.

Choose Your Victim

When you eventually enter the woods, saw in hand, it may be hard to see the trees for the forest. Which one should you fell?

First, waste no wealth. Prices obviously vary, but as a general rule the hardwoods are the most valuable, and some species such as black walnut always go for a premium. A tree is well on its way to becoming valuable timber if it's straight, the first crotch (where branches meet the trunk) is high up, and there are no visible injuries (broken branches, lightning scars, and the like) or disease (fungus on the trunk, beech cankers, and so on).

If a tree is more than 6 feet in circumference, it's got some value. Save it for a logger. There will be plenty of other trees to cull, which will improve the stand and eventually produce more valuable timber. As the old-

READING THE WOODS

In his book *Reading the Forested Landscape*, Tom Wessels takes a downright forensic approach to walking in the woods. His book can help a person of any level of expertise see more in a square foot of the forest than he thought possible.

A forest ecologist by training, Wessels teaches foresters how to read the landscape in order to understand its function as an ecosystem. "I work a lot with foresters, helping them see the forest from a larger landscape point of view, rather than just a stand-by-stand view," he says. "I also try to help them see a forest as an integrated system whose health and productivity can be maintained and enhanced only by understanding the functioning of the system."

I spent a week on the Appalachian Trail one summer after reading Mr. Wessels's book, to try to determine what I could about the woods around me. I learned to read not only how long ago a particular stone wall fenced in something other than trees, but also what kind of agriculture took place in the fields on either side. I learned to read the age of a variety of stumps and to determine how long beavers have been in or away from a particular spot. By learning to read their own forest, landowners can learn a great deal about how to manage their woods. Any reader of Wessels's book should be able to ramble out into his or her woodlot and quickly evaluate how and when it was last logged and whether any major fires or blowdowns have occurred there in the past.

Wessels encourages landowners to approach the future of their woodlots with an ecological sensibility. "Our forests provide an incredible array of ecosystem services that would be impossible to replace," he says. "An important one is water purification and recharge of the water table." He also emphasizes that, although wood can be harvested without disrupting the forest ecosystem, the best way for homeowners to save natural resources is to make their homes as energy efficient as possible. "Something as simple as passive solar heating would save huge amounts of oil and trees," he says.

timers say, "Sell the best, burn the rest." Since timber prices fluctuate, it is best to consult a forester or your local Cooperative Extension Service for advice on which species are most valuable locally.

Second, don't tackle more than you can handle safely (see "Size Matters," page 12).

Health

Selecting which tree to cut is obviously one of the primary forest-management decisions. Culling is tree breeding, in a sense. We leave the best specimens to reproduce and take the less desirable ones home to the stove, where they burn just as warm.

Look for trees with dead branches (hint: no leaves), split bark, or broken tops. If the growing tip of the tree is broken, the tree won't grow tall and straight but rather will "bush out" and shade out a lot of saplings. Storms do a good deal of this pruning. These trees are good candidates for the woodpile.

Thinning

Trees that are too close together won't reach their full potential as timber either, so go ahead and thin them out, leaving the straightest ones. There is a formula for determining the necessary distance between any two good-size trees. Estimate the average trunk diameter in inches of the two trees. To that figure, add six. The resulting number is the minimum distance, in feet, that should be between the

Take your pick. The large tree at the center-right of this photo could be felled for cordwood. Because it's so large and straight, however, it may become valuable timber at some point. An alternative would be to take down the smaller trees around it, to give the bigger tree room to grow.

two trees. If they are too close, one has to go. Since we're after firewood, we would probably cut the larger tree. If your goal is timber, harvest the smaller tree for firewood.

Your woodlot may well be full of three- or even four-stemmed specimens. Each stem is definitely in competition with its conjoined brothers. Leave the best-looking one and take the more horizontal brethren; they're just shading potentially more valuable neighbors.

Don't take out all the saplings between your big timber prospects. The forest needs the trees as much as we need the forest. The saplings are the future, of course, but in the present they help to shade the soil in the woods. If the soil is exposed to too much sunlight, it will dry out more than it should. Too much wind also dries the soil. An overly empty woodlot allows shrubs and invasive newcomers to compete with the very hardwood species we are trying to promote. (In our neck of the woods, a clear-cut creates what loggers call a "laurel hell" — a dense stand of mountain laurel shrubs that's nearly impossible to hack your way through.)

As you calculate the number of trees you'll need, remember that you must sometimes fell a smaller tree or two to clear the felling path of the tree you want.

Species

You don't have to be an expert woodsman to know which species of tree to cut, but you do have to know more than the son of a rich uncle I know who inspected the work of some landscapers he had hired. He had requested a border of white pines to separate his property from the neighbor's. The next week when he visited the construction site, he found a row of short wooden stakes driven into the ground every 20 feet or so, to mark the eventual location of the pines. I can still seem him there in the blustery March morning, staring at a construction stake set stubbornly a foot or so out of the ground. He looked and looked and then summoned the construction foreman over.

"Oh, Frawn-ciss," he drawled, "when will it *sprout*?"

Don't worry; with our help you'll soon know more than Cousin Rich.

As you can see from the table in the appendix, species vary considerably in their Btu (British thermal unit) content (see page 152). Hardwoods are where the heat is; they burn longer and release more heat, so we will concentrate on them. However, the softwoods,

---

Best Bets

So, which trees make the best firewood? See the table on page 152. Here is a rough list by species.

Excellent (20 million or more Btu per cord)

Apple, ash (white and Oregon), beech (yellow), birch, hickory, ironwood, maple (sugar, rock, or hard), oak

Good (18–19 million Btu per cord)

Birch (white), hackberry, larch or tamarack, maple (red or swamp)

Fair (15–17 million Btu per cord)

Cherry (black), Douglas fir, hemlock (western)

Poor (14 million or less Btu per cord)

Alder, aspen (popple/poplar in the East and quaking aspen out West), cedar, cottonwood, fir (balsam), hemlock (eastern), pine, redwood, spruce

Dingles & Spinneys

There are a number of truly satisfying ways of referring to little clusters of trees; spinney, copse, coppice, thicket, and glen are but a few. My favorite term for a thicket is "dingle."

especially pines, have their uses. The finest pieces of split oak won't warm you if you can't get the suckers lit.

This is where the pines come in. They are resinous (sappy, smoky) and contribute to creosote formation in the stovepipe, so we don't burn them in bulk. However, they release a quick burst of flame and heat. Pine is ideal as a "first stick" on, right after the kindling and before the bigger pieces of hardwood. (Read more about building a fire in chapter 6, "Burn, Baby, Burn.") So don't completely spurn the pines. However, since they are slow to split (knotty) and destined for small pieces, don't fell any huge ones.

The "climax community" (sounds exciting!) in most Northeastern forests consists of ash, maple, beech, birch, and oak. The climax community is the population the forest naturally evolves toward. Fortunately, these are all good sources of firewood.

Pioneer species. White birches are among the first trees to colonize a stand of ground after a clear-cut.

The Rare "Cornmeal" Birch

Stephen

A friend of mine, Jake, was a good-time guy. You'd like him. He had a great-aunt, an aged unmarried tyrant who was rich and very proper. Jake always felt he didn't meet her high standards and, frankly, didn't go out of his way to visit her because he always felt inadequate.

So Jake kept on doing what he did: laughing and listening and playing sports and drinking beer and teaching school and seeing the good and accepting the bad in children and trying to help them. Jake was never one to judge, although he sometimes had difficulty in discerning.

Years passed and his great-aunt, after living to a very great (if not ripe) old age, died. The funeral left Jake feeling less than full, sort of lonesome for a past that seemed more like a future: full of what might have been. He wished he'd known his relative better, or perhaps that she had known him differently.

Jake went back home and back to work. A week or so later, his brother called him. These brothers weren't twins, but they might as well have been.

"They're breaking up Auntie's house," the brother said, "and we can have something."

So the brothers returned to the big house the next weekend. It was just about empty by now. They poked around upstairs and in a wing where the maids had lived in the old days, but they didn't find much. Finally, they worked their way down cellar and there they struck pay dirt. In the old coal cellar, they found a trove of beautiful white birch logs.

"All right," said Jake. "The president of my college had a fireplace in his office that was always laid with three clean pieces of white birch. Very tasteful."

"Even better, they're aged to perfection. Good dry firewood," said Bro.

They loaded up their vans and when Jake arrived back home, he called up his good friend, Steve (that's me), who had a chain saw.

"Come over tomorrow," Jake said, "and saw up these logs so they'll fit in my woodstove."

"You don't have a woodstove," I pointed out.

"Are you kidding? With a supply of free firewood? I just ordered one."

I hustled over there after work the next day, packing my McCulloch. In the driveway was the van full of white birch logs. A sawhorse was set up behind it, with the first log resting there waiting to be cut.

"Uh, Jake, that birch is going to be . . ."

"Fire that mother up! Let's make ourselves some stove wood."

Twenty or thirty short pulls later, the McCulloch leapt to life.

I laid the whirling teeth on the birch and — poof! — it exploded into powder finer than johnnycake meal. Jake had unwittingly brought home a van full of ancestral dust.

Those tight birch wrappers had long ago dry-rotted the classic firewood. If you don't burn birch in one or two years, it gets mighty punky.

Trees I Have Burned

Alder: Firewood source out West. But at only 14 million Btu per cord, it makes a Yankee grateful for maple.

Apple: The cook's favorite for flavor, apple makes good firewood because it burns so hot.

Ash: Of the hardwoods, ash is last to unfurl its leaves and first to drop them. It's straight grained and easy to split and dries quickly.

Aspen: I call it popple. It's pretty, but it's also pretty sorry cordwood.

Beech: The beech is a stubborn hardwood. It just doesn't want to go down and is seemingly able to hold itself up by the merest twig, when by all rights and woodcraft it ought to be timbering. The beech's busy fingers also seem to snag more belt loops, whip more eyeballs, and generally add injury to obstruction in the woodlot. It has skin like an elephant and a memory just as long. There is a good side, though: Beech is actually one of our better sources of heat.

Birch: White, yellow, gray, black, and paper birch all grow fast and pretty and die young. They pack decent firewood in an attractive wrapper.

Cherry: Sometimes straight as a rail, sometimes crooked as a _____ (insert occupation or political party here), cherry has rough bark and orange wood that raise human spirits and warm our hearths.

Elm: Old-timers have an apparently irrational mania about the elm. There are rhymes about what a pisser it is to split and how little heat it bequeaths. I am here to report to you that this prejudice is entirely justified. Elm will eat your axes and your mauls, your wedges and your labor. It will warm you twice in the woodlot, but precious little in the living room.

Hemlock: I hate to say anything on God's earth isn't worth the effort. Maybe we'll leave it at this: God didn't put hemlock in your woodpile, so why should you?

Hickory: What's good for the barbecue is good for the woodstove.

Hornbeam: Known as hop or American hornbeam, muscle wood, and ironwood, the tree contains very hard wood. It burns well when dry.

Locust: The dense bark demands extra drying time, but once locust is dry it is light and oily and throws serious heat. (Like Pedro Martinez. Just kidding; locusts don't have Jeri curls.)

Maple: The staple of the diet of the typical New England stove is maple. Red maple, also known as swamp maple and other more derogatory terms, contains considerably less heat than its cousin, the sugar maple, so you need to be able to tell them apart. You might guess this by hefting a piece of each when first cut: The sugar maple is denser and heavier.

Mesquite: It burns sweet and hot.

Oak: It's the good stuff: dense, heavy, and full of Btus. Oaks come in red, white, scarlet, black, and pin (stripe).

Pine: White pine has the soft needles that remind me of Christmas; long-leaf and pitch pines have lots of resin; ponderosa pine reaches huge heights. I used to cut lots of pulpwood; the pages of this book might be pine, in fact. These are all important virtues, but not to be confused with firewood. The high resin content will start a fire, for sure. But burning a whole load of it will leave a coating of creosote in your chimney, increasing your chances of chimney fire.

Walnut: Don't burn tomorrow's furniture today.

Don't Go Whole Hog

A forester by the name of Lincoln Fish (see page 56) once told us that cutting too aggressively around young, straight trees to try to give them room might expose them to too much direct sunlight. The thin bark of these younger trees is designed to make the most of the light filtering through the canopy. If this canopy is cleared too quickly and thoroughly, the young trees will get sunstroke. Wind is another problem. Anywhere a large tree goes down, the trees around it will suffer incidental damage from increased exposure.

Locked in a strange struggle, trees both compete with and rely on one another. Each has to make sacrifices in stability and branch distribution in order to keep reaching and expanding for light. When a tree loses a neighbor, it is immediately unbalanced and over-extended on that particular side, and it will frequently suffer somewhat for this imbalance before it can begin to reap the benefits of the new real estate.

Size Matters

As we will explain later (see chapter 3 for advice on choosing and felling trees), you have a number of important choices to make before you rev up that Husky.

1. Do you really want to do this? Cutting firewood is *not* a test of your manhood. It's just a cheap way of heating your house, and no one should get hurt doing it. So if you have doubts, listen to them.

2. Are you sober? Never pick up a saw after so much as a single sip of beer. And this is being written by one of a long line of beer guzzlers. Of course, this goes for drugs, recreational and otherwise. (Remember that line on the cough-syrup bottle about operating machinery?)

3. If the wind is strong, beware.

4. If there is a heavy snow load on the branches, beware.

5. And, last, Paul Bunyan: If the tree is more than 70 feet tall or 6 feet in circumference, it is best left alone. It's too big for a beginner. Learn on smaller trees, and work your way up. Also, such trees are big enough for the sawmill, and you might be burning valuable timber in an attempt to save on the fuel bill.

Sweat the small stuff. For cleaning up minor storm damage like this broken sapling, a simple pruning saw will do the job.

Big blue. A large butt log, with much taper.

Bull bucker. Man in charge of fallers and buckers.

Bullcook. The chore boy around camp. He cuts fuel, fills wood boxes, sweeps bunkhouses, feeds pigs, and is often the butt of camp jokes.

Corks. Calks; short, sharp spikes set in the soles of shoes.

Dehorn. Any sort of booze. Used by old-time Wobblies to denote anything that takes the mind of the worker from the class struggle.

Donkey. Stationary engine.

Donkey doctor. Donkey-engine mechanic.

Driving pitch. High water suitable for driving logs down a river.

Flunkey. Same as *cookee*. Cookhouse help.

Gandy dancer. Pick-and-shovel man.

Hair-pounder. A horse teamster.

Hoot-nanny. A small device used to hold a crosscut saw while sawing a log from underneath.

Ink slinger. A logging-camp timekeeper.

Long logger. A logger in the fir and redwood country of the West Coast. So called because logs are cut as long as 40 feet.

"Make her out." What a logger tells the timekeeper when he wants his paycheck. "I'm quitting." Sometimes "Mix me a walk" is used instead.

Nosebag show. A camp where midday meal is taken to the woods in lunch buckets.

Packing a card. Mean's he's a union man.

Powder monkey. Man in charge of blasting operations.

River hog. A name for river drivers.

Rolled. Robbed while drunk.

Sawdust eater. One of those fellers who works in a sawmill.

Scaler. The fellow who says how much lumber a log contains. His rule stick is said to be the *cheat stick*.

Schoolmarm. A crotched log, consisting mostly of two trunks.

Skidroad. In the old days a road over which oxen pulled logs. Today it means that part of a city where loggers congregate when in town. As such, its meaning approximates *bowery*.

Sky hooker. Top man in a sleigh-loading crew.

String of flats. Flatcars; griddle cakes.

Swedish fiddle. Crosscut saw.

Whistle punk. The boy who blows signals for the yarding crew.

Widow maker. Tree or branch blown down by wind.

Windfall bucker. A man who is engaged in sawing up trees that have been blown down by wind.

Wobbly. A member of the Industrial Workers of the World.

Yarding. The assembling of logs.

— excerpted from *Holy Old Mackinaw: A Natural History of the American Lumberjack,* by Stewart H. Holbrook, published in 1938.

Best Bets for Btus

Here's a sampling of some of the best cordwood money (or your own sweat) can buy.

Apple

26.5 million Btus

Ash

19.1 million Btus

Beech

24 million Btus

Birch (white)

20.3 million Btus

Birch (yellow)

23.6 million Btus

Black locust

26.8 million Btus

Cherry

20 million Btus

Hickory

27.7 million Btus

Ironwood (hop hornbeam)

27.3 million Btus

Red oak

24 million Btus

Sugar maple

24 million Btus

Tamarack

20.8 million Btus

2 Get Your GEAR

OLD-TIME LUMBERJACKS didn't have a lot of complicated machinery. With just an ax and a saw they managed to bring down more massive timber than anyone today is allowed to cut. Most people felling trees today (on a small scale) use a chain saw, which chews through the wood a fair bit faster than the old two-man saw. A chain saw can also be a lot more dangerous, however, and it needs at least rudimentary maintenance to keep it operating safely and efficiently.

Choosing a Saw

If you are interested in harvesting wood from your land to burn, be it a half cord for a decorative fireplace or nine cords for a drafty house, you'll want to look into getting a chain saw. It may seem quite pricey to the first-time buyer, but you need to keep a few things in mind. A good chain saw is an amazing tool. It is an engine that can run upside down at twenty below, cranking over 5,000 rpm, for over a half hour without stopping. It can allow you to turn a standing, 20-inch-diameter maple into rounds ready to be split in under an hour. All it asks in return is very simple maintenance. Unless you are simply pruning and cleaning in your woods, you will need a chain saw of some kind to process any amount of firewood. With the exception of an old Parker Brothers 20-gauge shotgun, my saw is the toughest, most reliable tool (with moving parts) that I have ever owned.

Each gunslinger his gun, each bluesman his guitar, each redneck his truck. The last of these comparisons may be the most appropriate, as the Stihl/Husqvarna debate remains as lively in some circles as the Ford/Chevy conundrum does in others. Actually, they're pretty much the same circles. I'll get the prejudices out of the way early by saying that I drive a Ford pickup and use a Stihl 039, which I received as my college graduation gift from my father, the Husqvarna user. There's more sense to the man than I often admit. Stihl saws win out in a contest of power-to-weight ratio, and they run at a very high rpm. Husqvarna saws ("Husky" if you're in a shop) have more power for the money, as well as a larger fuel capacity. Each starts well in the cold and has winter and summer settings, which regulate airflow for the conditions that are particular to each season.

As I've said before, the most important consideration when buying a saw is how much wood you're going to cut each year. Any figure you arrive at below 10 cords could be handled by a saw with a 3- to 4-brake horsepower (bhp) engine and a 16- to 20-inch bar. Such a saw would weigh around 13 pounds.

Saw weight Thirteen pounds may not sound like a helluva lot, but it is enough to wear an inexperienced user right out. The 19-ounce fuel capacity will be your best friend in this case, as you won't be able to cut for more than 40 minutes without having to refuel. Let me say it again because you can-

not hear it too much: Do not continue cutting when your muscles are so tired that they are approaching failure. You need to stop as soon as you feel yourself taking little shortcuts, letting the saw droop close to your body.

Bar Size When deciding what size bar to get on a saw, the power of the saw and the kind of wood to be cut are the two most important factors. For instance, most manufacturers sell a midsize saw that will accommodate a bar up to 20 inches long, which is fine for cutting pulpwood, such as spruce or white pine. If the wood you'll be burning is primarily hardwood and the trees are in the neighborhood of 2 feet in diameter, then a midsize saw outfitted with a 16-inch bar is fine. The longer the bar, the more teeth the saw has to drag through the wood at once, and a 20-inch bar would likely put unhealthy stress on the engine, not to mention your body.

You should be able to heft your saw easily with one hand and run it for 10 minutes without becoming exhausted. It's one thing to get some monster with a 30-inch bar, an hour's worth of fuel, and dogs big enough to skewer badgers just because it will look cool sitting on your tailgate. But if you can't throw it around and run it all day, you won't get any wood in your shed.

Anatomy of a Chain Saw

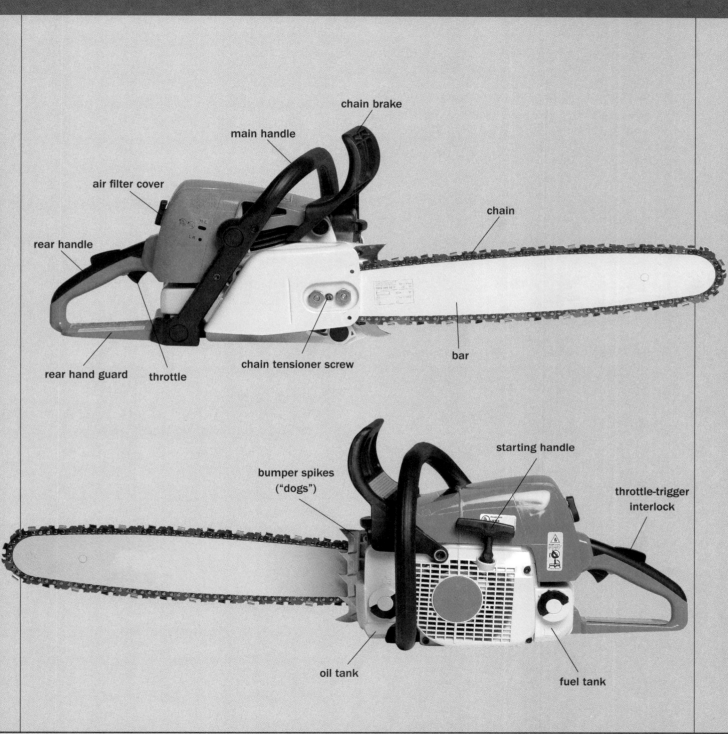

chain brake

main handle

air filter cover

chain

rear handle

rear hand guard

throttle

chain tensioner screw

bar

starting handle

bumper spikes ("dogs")

throttle-trigger interlock

oil tank

fuel tank

Rev It Up

To start the saw, put the run/stop switch in the run position and the choke in the start setting as. On most saws, this produces a very fast-running, loud start. Don't expect the engine to begin at an idle. Chain saws roar to life going full bore. For this reason, you need to make sure that nothing is near the chain. Not your legs or sleeves or saplings or rocks or other equipment — nothing. Place the saw on solid ground, preferably on a small mound, so that when you put your right foot in the handle, it lifts the bar up away from the ground. Brace your left hand firmly on the nontrigger handle, the metal bar that your left hand will be spending its days with, and give the pull handle a good hard pull. The saw should either start right up or give a promising cough and start on the second pull. At this point, remove your foot and pick up the saw to give the trigger a light squeeze and allow the engine to move back down to an idle before you start cutting wood.

Some people will suggest starting the saw with the chain brake engaged. In my experience, this just hampers the saw's ability to fire up. The idle speed should be such that the saw doesn't burst into a full-throttle roar when the engine catches but, rather, comes to life at a safe idle.

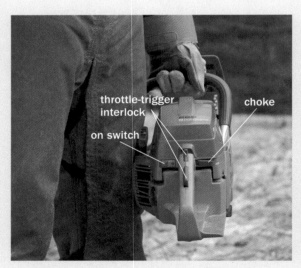

throttle-trigger interlock

choke

on switch

1 Before you can rev it up, the saw needs to be turned on (that should be a no-brainer). Also, the choke has to be out, and the throttle-trigger interlock should be engaged.

2 A chain saw should always be started on level ground, clear of any rocks, logs, legs, or other impediments. Stabilize the saw by slipping your foot through the rear handle and holding the main handle firmly with one hand.

On the safe side. Many foresters recommend engaging the chain brake before starting the saw, especially if you're just learning to use a chain saw. With the chain brake engaged, only the engine (not the chain) will start up when you pull the starting handle. When you're about to start sawing, you can then disengage the chain brake and let it fly.

If the saw keeps putting your left hand to sleep, don't worry; just make sure to stop often enough that you are not putting yourself in danger with fatigue and weakness. When you are tired or focusing on pain in your limbs, your attention is not where it should be.

3 Let 'er rip! Pull the starting handle (hopefully just once or twice) to bring the saw to life.

One final note, and then I'll stop nagging: It may not seem necessary to mention this, but do not run a chain saw in a closed, unventilated area for any length of time. Because the saw has a two-stroke engine, it runs dirtier than a car engine and can fill an area like a basement, barn, or garage with exhaust very quickly. Why on earth would someone do this, you ask? I was building a wood rack in my house because there was no garage and 3 feet of snow on the ground outside. I had the clever idea of making the rack in the cellar. Not having my circular saw at hand, I decided to make the series of relatively precise cuts necessary with the chain saw. This worked about as well as you might imagine, and my increasing dizziness caused what was initially a tolerance of plus or minus ⅛ inch to rocket up to "plus-or-minus-one-foot-as-long-as-it's-not-my-foot." All joking aside, you should be very aware of ventilation when using a saw. If you get dizzy from the exhaust fumes, you increase your chances of lopping off some valuable part of your body. This is to be avoided.

Buck 'em up. Anytime you're operating a chain saw, you should wear appropriate safety gear to protect yourself from flying debris, falling limbs, the high decibels of a running saw, and the possibility of a random slip of the chain saw near your legs.

The "rule of no thumb" dictates that you should never attempt to tighten the chain on your chain saw while it is running.

Operation Checklist

First of all, make sure that your saw has enough gasoline. Chain saws have what is known as a two-stroke engine, as opposed to the four-stroke engine in your car. A two-stroke engine runs faster and more powerfully than a four-stroke, but it has different lubrication needs as a result. Chain-saw gas needs oil mixed directly in with it. Buy yourself some of this additive oil at any hardware store, and read the mixing ratios on the back.

Make sure your saw also has enough bar and chain oil. This too can be picked up in a hardware store, or in any country store worth its weight in Slim Jims. The bar and chain oil goes in the other big tank on your saw. The gas tank and the bar and chain oil tank are marked clearly. Depending on the temperature while you're working, you will want a specific bar and chain oil. Most places carry both summer- and winter-weight oil. The summer oil is thicker because the higher summer running temperature of the saw requires oil with a higher viscosity. The bar and chain oil is dispensed directly onto the bar inside the housing. In order to make sure that this is happening, once the saw is running aim the blade down at a clean patch of snow, or other light-colored surface if it's summer or you're in a mild-winter climate, and throttle all the way up. You should see a fine spray of oil spitting off the tip of the bar. It is very important not to let the oil reservoir run dry, as the friction

SWEET WOODSMAN

Frannie Wells was a Renaissance man, Jefferson's ideal: the educated yeoman farmer. He was a dairy farmer, a selectman, a guide for geology classes from neighboring colleges, and a sugar maker extraordinaire. Frannie would generously lend his cordwood saw every fall to travel around the neighborhood, where groups of three or four guys would hook it to a tractor and buck up the stove wood, one house at a time.

Frannie was my hero and my neighbor, but also my boss for several sugaring seasons. He taught me to tap trees. And we cut wood together. It takes lots of wood to fuel the ravenous evaporators that boil the water out of the sap. Since 40 to 60 gallons of sap yield one gallon of syrup, Frannie went through cord after cord to produce 250 to 500 gallons of syrup each spring.

Frannie and I would ride around the woods on his tractor, pulling a funny old homemade wagon (a "cob-job"). When we came to a pile — and he had them everywhere, up hill and down, and in the swamps — I'd jump off and begin to load the wagon. I remember heaving one huge butt log onto the wagon before he could arrive to help me. I felt very proud when Frannie shook his head and marveled, "Young and strong." But, that night and ever since I have remembered the elegiac, soft tone of his voice and wondered who was the young, strong man he was thinking of. Another time we were racketing down a slope in the woods, near the ledges. There on his little logging track was a piece of wood that had probably bounced off the last load the year before. This time Frannie brought tractor and wagon to a slewing stop on the steep terrain, set the emergency brake, and pounced on the errant wood before I had so much as moved. He tossed the piece into the wagon and blushed. "Probably nobody else in the world would stop for that," he said. "Guess I *am* a Yankee."

He was, at that, but I'll also remember him for always selling 13 ears of corn for the price of a dozen, "just in case," and never mowing hay till the meadowlarks were through nesting. The result? Late, woody hay and the legend of the late, dearly lamented Frannie Wells.

along the groove in the bar would quickly take the temper out of the metal, weakening it.

Check the chain to make sure it isn't too loose; you should be able to pull the chain up (or down) off the bar just far enough that you could slip the edge of a dime between the teeth and the bar. When they are new, chains will stretch much more than you can imagine, so stop periodically and turn off the saw to check the tension. Stihl saws have made the leap to easy tightening by mounting the chain tensioner screw on the side of the saw, right where the bar is bolted to the saw. Use the wrench/screwdriver tool that came with the saw to loosen the two nuts holding the bar, then simply twist the tensioner screw clockwise to tighten the chain. Remember to retighten the nuts holding the bar, or all will be for naught. On other brands of saws, such as Jonsered and Husqvarna, the tensioner screw is a little harder to get at (see page 26).

Working on the Chain, Gang

Chain tightening and sharpening are so frequently necessary on any saw that everyone needs to know how to perform these tasks in the field. Chains can shrink and expand with use, air temperature, and their own temperature, so a chain that's been tightened and used one day may need to be adjusted again in short order.

Unless the chain is so loose that it seems in danger of coming off the bar, or so tight that it cannot be run around the bar by hand, it may be easiest to fire up the saw, let the engine warm for a minute, turn off the saw, then determine whether the chain needs adjustment. A loose chain (see page 26) will hang from the bar of the saw in a noticeable way.

Whichever brand of chain saw you buy, it's important that it have a very accessible chain tensioner screw. The tensioner screw forces the bar away from the sprocket that drives the chain. Inevitably the bar slips back a little, and the chain stretches out a little. ("A little" here is in mechanical terms. Hacks out there may

---

Chain Saw Dos . . .

➤ Always wear safety gear: chaps, ear protection, helmet, steel-toed boots.
➤ Always start the chain saw on the ground.
➤ Sharpen the chain with a jig at the end of each extended use.
➤ Take the chain saw to a professional to be sharpened after every fifth home sharpening.
➤ Clean the air filter and check the chain oil before starting the saw.

. . . and Taboos

➤ Never run a saw above shoulder height.
➤ Never operate a chain saw while standing on a ladder or other elevated spot.
➤ Don't run a chain saw after drinking or taking cough syrup or any other sedative.
➤ Don't run a chain saw when you're tired.

1 The chain on a saw should be touched up before each use. This can be done at home with a jig made especially for this purpose.

cutting edge

2 The highlighted edges of the cutting teeth shown above are the surfaces that actually bite into the wood — the edges that need sharpening.

not believe in dimensions less than 1/16 inch, but they might believe in such things when a chain comes loose.)

The "rule of no thumb" dictates that you should never attempt to determine this adjustment while the saw is running, even at an innocent idle. Frannie Wells, a neighboring farmer (see page 23), ended up with only one thumb from a mistake made in a situation like this, and I have spent many an idle moment wondering where in the woods that little skeletal crew of bones, with saw marks and gnaw marks, finally settled.

Sharpening a chain is tricky and exacting enough that after every five touch-ups or so, it should be done by a professional. The reason is that even with a little jig at home, it is difficult to file down the cutting teeth and depth gauges evenly all the way along the chain. A good jig costs about the same as a sharpening in a shop, and in 5 minutes you can have a chain that really rips every day.

3 The two flat bars on the outside of the jig guide the file and maintain a proper angle during sharpening. The part of the jig that does the actual sharpening is a rounded file that fits into the groove of the cutting tooth.

4 For the rounded file to fit properly into the groove of the cutting tooth, the jig should be held at a 45-degree angle to the chain.

sharpening a chain

a loose chain will hang off the bar

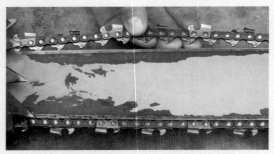

1 Chains will do much more stretching than you would imagine when they're new, so stop the saw periodically while you're working to check the tension. This chain is clearly too loose.

Cleaning a Chain Saw

There are a few more simple maintenance procedures that even the most ham-handed of Luddites can execute. (You may not know us, but anyone you come across with a toolbox full of bent wrenches and hands covered with cuts is a good stand-in.) Before every trip to the woodlot you should pull the air filter and scrub the clotted sawdust free, using an old toothbrush dipped in gasoline. Any saw you buy will have a manual that details the location of each part.

If your saw does not fire up after just a few pulls, the spark plugs may have become dirty. Scrubbing the gap between the insulator nose and the electrodes with a wire brush and solvent can help get rid of the gunk. The head of

2 Start by loosening the two nuts that hold the bar onto the engine housing. The wrench/screwdriver tool pictured comes with the chain saw.

3 Locate the tensioner screw. On Husqvarna chain saws, the screw is located at the base of the bar, on the engine housing. On a Stihl saw, the screw is right on the side of the housing.

the electrode, the side closer to the body of the plug, can be refiled so that the electrode is freed of grime and squared off again.

I have spoken only of Husqvarna and Stihl because those are the two saws I know best, but we still run an old Jonsered, and it works just fine. Dad had a heavy old McCulloch that he used for years and years, so if you find a good deal out there, don't be completely dominated by my prejudice, though most of the loggers I know run Stihl or Husqvarna saws. Some loggers in the Pacific Northwest used to run Homelite saws for heavy-duty work. The main point is not to buy a cheap saw. The saw you get will be subject to extremely harsh working conditions, and you'll need it to start up reliably and operate safely each time.

Tips for First-Timers

➤ Chain saws are quite awkwardly balanced. To stabilize the saw while you're working on it, use a C-clamp to pinch the floor of the trigger handle to a workbench.
➤ When touching up the chain, you may have to put the bar in a vice. Make sure the vice is gripping the bar itself, and not pinching the chain.
➤ New chains can be quite sharp, so handling with gloves is recommended.
➤ An old toothbrush is excellent for cleaning hard-to-reach places on the saw.
➤ Check the pull cord for fraying at the spot where it meets the pull handle. This is the spot that wears the fastest, and if you yank the handle off, the cord wraps up inside and is a pain to free. To avoid this, cut the cord at the frayed spot, pull it through the handle, and tie it in a knot.

4 To tighten the chain, use the screwdriver end of the tool to twist the tensioner screw clockwise. Remember to follow up by tightening the nuts that hold the bar.

5 After tightening the chain, you should be able to pull the chain off the bar to the extent that you could slip a dime between the teeth and the bar.

Chaps Aren't Just for Cowboys

One evening in the middle of the winter when I was 12 years old, I was indoors, ostensibly doing some homework. My father was out back a few hundred yards, trying to wring the last bit of work out of February dusk. This is already a bad idea with a chain saw. One needs the best possible visibility for good footing and a clear sense of what the work looks like and where potential stresses lie in the wood to be cut. If this had been the extent of his risk taking, I would have nothing to report.

My father's goal in the gloaming was to cut back some of the dense underbrush that had recently begun to choke the banks of a small pond in the back field. The real stroke of genius came when he realized that the job would be far easier while the pond was frozen solid. This makes a bit of ragged sense on the face of it, but most would shy away from chain-saw work after sundown on ice. Here's why: As he made his way around the deeply frozen perimeter, he let the tip of the running saw dip down near his knee just as his foot slipped a little. He was so cold, and so intent on finishing, that it was only as warmth spread down his leg that he realized the tug he'd felt had been the saw in his knee, and not a branch snagging him. A 45-minute car ride and a number of stitches later, he decided to get some chaps.

A good brand of protective leggings contains Prolar, a product similar to Kevlar, which is found in many high-end protective products, such as flak jackets. These fibers snarl in the chain and clump instantly in the sprocket and dogs of a running saw. Product safety guidelines require that chaps halt a chain moving at 2,600 feet per minute. The brands I researched made claims as high as 3,000 feet per minute.

Protect Your Head

In addition to keeping your legs intact, it's a good idea to protect yourself from flying splinters, falling limbs, and the deafening howl of the chain saw. Whenever you're operating a chain saw, you should always wear some kind of eye protection: safety glasses or, better yet, a face shield. And those dangling limbs high up in the tree? They're called "widowmakers" for a reason. Wearing a helmet may save your life.

Being cut by the saw and hit by flying objects are pretty visible ways of hurting yourself,

Be hardheaded. This all-in-one helmet also features a face shield and earmuffs.

Gearing Up for Safety

The eyes have it. You can't fell trees if you've been blinded by flying splinters, so protect your eyes with a pair of safety goggles.

All in one. We both use this handy helmet, which provides ear, head, and eye protection all in one.

A hard head. If you're not taking down trees but you're in a forest where someone else is, you'll want the protection of a helmet and some earplugs.

What's that? Chain saws run at a high decibel level; earmuffs or earplugs are a must for avoiding hearing damage.

Get a grip. Gloves protect your hands from flying splinters and give you a better grip on the saw.

Logger leggings. These chaps are made of Prolar, a fabric that can stop a running chain in seconds flat (before it digs into your leg, in other words).

but many people forget the hearing damage that chain saws can cause. Most saws escalate beyond 100 decibels when running flat out. This is far more than enough noise to damage not only the operator's hearing, but also the hearing of anyone within a 100-foot radius. Hearing damage can happen very quickly, and it is permanent. A good rule is that if you must shout to be heard over another noise, that noise is at a damaging level. Anytime you operate a chain saw, be sure to wear earplugs or earmuffs.

Some manufacturers sell a tough, lightweight helmet with hearing protection and a face mask. Considering the alternative of tinnitus (permanent ringing in your ears), damaged eyes, or a hard blow to the head, helmets are a bargain. A plastic mesh mask is lighter and cheaper than a metal screen, and nothing has broken through mine yet. The helmets are not rated for protection in the case of a motorcycle accident, bear attack, or falling anvil.

Maul in the Family

For years my father and I used the classic wood maul to split wood. All of these (and I say "these" because we went through dozens) consisted of a hardwood (hickory or ash) shaft and an 8- to 12-pound head. The weight of the head is usually stamped crudely into the bottom of the poll (the "poll" is any portion of the nonsplitting or non-

Sharp contrast. A maul (above left) is different from an ax (above right) in more ways than one. Mauls are big, heavy, and not as sharp; they're used for splitting up large pieces of wood. Axes are smaller and sharper and are generally used only for splitting small pieces of kindling.

cutting side of an ax or maul head). The heads on these wood-handled mauls had an exaggerated flare to their blades. By this I mean that along the top and the bottom of the head, approaching the blade, the head flares both up and down, so that the blade itself is a gentle curve 2 inches taller than the height of the head where it meets the handle. This gives the maul much more versatility in the angle at which it can strike the wood, but with this you lose out on pounds-per-square-inch force at the moment of impact. The heavier, straight-bladed mauls we use now are not as elegant or delicate, but those two words are as pearls before swine when confronted with heaps of knotted maple rounds.

When choosing a maul you should realize that even the most experienced of cordwood heroes will eventually break the conventional wood-handled maul, even when it is equipped with one of those stop-gap rubber collars (which, in my experience, simply make the inevitable into a scary surprise). There are many varieties of fiberglass-handled mauls on the market, and though they do tend to outlast the wooden variety, they are impossible to retrofit once shattered. On the other hand,

the desperate wood burner can often simply shorten a broken handle with the delicate application of a drawknife, plane, or rudimentary lathe. Both options have their advantages and drawbacks, and so are fertile ground for hardware-store gossips.

A handle usually breaks because of a combination of mistakes. The first of these is overshooting the wood to be split and striking it with the top of the handle rather than the blade. The second is from persistent levering of the handle while the head is stuck in a round of troublesome wood. The long handle of a maul allows for tremendous leverage when the head becomes stuck, but this same

Wedging the big fellas. Start the wedge in any available crack with a few gentle taps, then stand back and give it hell.

Tools for Timber

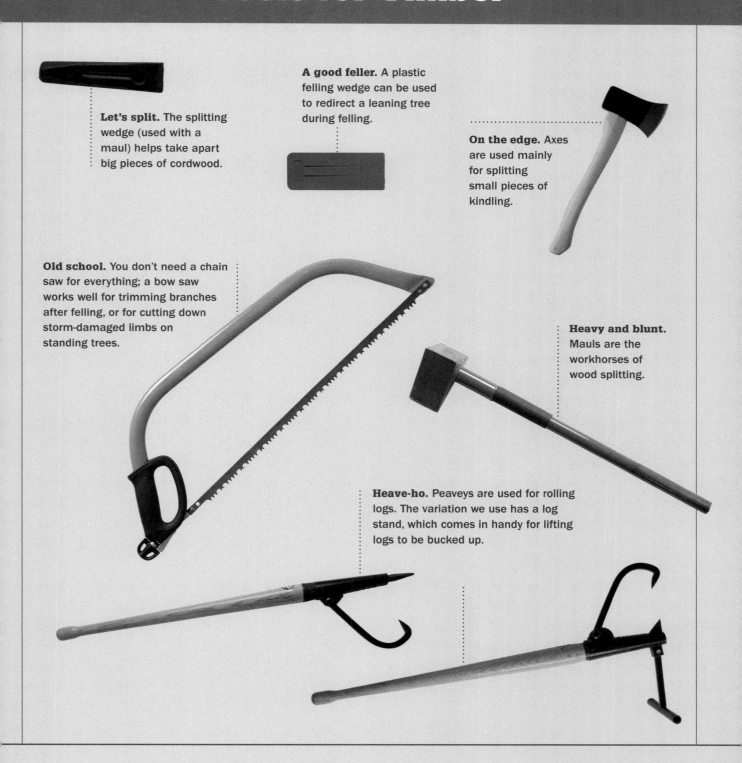

Let's split. The splitting wedge (used with a maul) helps take apart big pieces of cordwood.

A good feller. A plastic felling wedge can be used to redirect a leaning tree during felling.

On the edge. Axes are used mainly for splitting small pieces of kindling.

Old school. You don't need a chain saw for everything; a bow saw works well for trimming branches after felling, or for cutting down storm-damaged limbs on standing trees.

Heavy and blunt. Mauls are the workhorses of wood splitting.

Heave-ho. Peaveys are used for rolling logs. The variation we use has a log stand, which comes in handy for lifting logs to be bucked up.

leverage destroys the integrity of the fibers just below the head. If the maul becomes stuck fast in a round, so that a sharp blow from the heel of your hand will not free it, refrain from wrenching the handle, but rather tap the poll to and fro with anything handy and let the blade walk itself out. If your maul gets stuck in a piece again and again, set that piece aside for the bonfire. If you're not planning a bonfire but do have a chain saw, then score a deep cross into the cut face of the log and try splitting it along these artificial cracks.

> "Yanking a pinched maul from a piece of wood is . . . obnoxious."

When a maul or ax handle finally, and inevitably, does break, it can be difficult to get the remainder of the handle out of the eye. When dealing with a stubborn maul in this predicament, we have just tossed it in the stove and burned the handle out. Do not do this with an ax, as the heat in your woodstove may take the temper out of the relatively delicate blade. Sometimes the handle can be pounded out from the bottom; the wedge in the top prevents pounding it out from the opposite direction. If this proves too difficult, try the following: Drill a number of holes down through the handle to take the pressure out, and drive the remaining wood free with an old carriage bolt and hammer. If all this fails, send the offending head to me with a self-addressed, stamped envelope and $75.

The Megamaul

The solution to the eternal maul-handle dilemma came to my father and me in the ugliest of packages (not to be disdained, as the stork that delivered W. C. Fields would have told you years later). My father was searching for something stronger, heavier, and cruder (a pursuit that has been a common thread in almost all of his material acquisitions), when he was given what we now refer to as the megamaul.

The megamaul weighed in the vicinity of 20 pounds when we got it, and a sight more after its three welding surgeries. It consisted of a large, blunt wedge at the end of a thick length of iron pipe. The advantages here were weight and the angle of attack. Conventional mauls, to say nothing of axes, have a relatively sharp, or acute, angle to their blades. Where these tools might come to a point of something like 5 to 15 degrees, the megamaul was between 20 and 25 degrees. This meant that it never, ever got stuck in a piece of wood. As you will all soon find out, yanking a pinched maul from a piece of wood is time-consuming, obnoxious, and damaging to the equipment.

There are 12- and 14-pound commercial versions of this maul available now, in striking red, and within the same price range as a more old-fashioned maul. Keeping in mind that you will not break this metal monster for the next 20 years, it's a bargain at twice the price. If you are of the right frame or disposition, a maul like this will save you time, frustration, and money. I offer only one caveat: These mauls are not so good as their more traditional brethren when it comes to driving splitting wedges through knotty pieces. If you have selected your trees carefully and bucked them up strategically, though, there should be very few pieces requiring the wedge treatment. If you have a fireplace or wood furnace, the rough customers may fit there without any more sweat wasted.

Hydraulic Splitters

I feel it incumbent upon me to tell you a little about the competition here: mechanized splitters. So that the next time you're up to your thighs in 10°F weather whaling away on some 18-inch rounds of stubborn beech — and loving every minute of it — you can give a wry smirk. There are all varieties of hydraulic splitters, from the small trailer-style ones that can be hauled around by trucks, tractors, or even ATVs on up to the top-of-the-line firewood processing machines. These warrant a mention, because unlike their tow-around relatives, they are complicated, unaffordable, and pretty damn cool. I know, I know, this is high treason, but only on the order of pining for something totally unattainable rather than a nicer car or an oil furnace.

I surrender. When you're ready to admit defeat, it may be time to drop a chunk of change on a hydraulic wood splitter. This one can be hooked up to a trailer hitch and towed behind a truck into the woods.

Packing a punch. Though we're staunchly in the "splitting by hand" camp, you have to admire the way a hydraulic splitter can tear through an ugly mother like this one.

One Wild Splitter

Frank

A mountain of a man named Charlie Sobasko lumbered out of the boiler room where he spent his days and found me mowing the grounds of the small college at which we both worked. He rumbled, "You look like you know how to work." I responded that I thought I did, and he offered me more than twice what the college was paying, under the table, to run his "firewood machine" after work each day.

The extra coin sounded good, and I knew this giant to be a character and a legendary worker. What he dismissed as a firewood machine could be yours, gentle reader, for fifty grand. Under experienced hands it can produce four cords an hour. Think on that for a moment. That is as much firewood as many of you will use in a whole winter, provided a tight house.

When I got to Charlie's house, he insisted on giving me the grand tour. He swept his paw at a low ranch with vinyl siding and said, "There's my house." We walked past this point of interest, and he again gestured broadly, this time at 3 acres of heaped logs in rough corridors. "There's the wood." He led me to a small shed I had missed in all the glitz and glamour and showed me the beast. His machine consisted of a ratty swiveling chair mounted on an expanded metal platform, with a view of the whole process. In front of the chair was a row of worn levers, each capped with a wad of tattered electrician's tape. Below the chair, and straight ahead, was a huge metal tray with three sets of dogged (spiked) chains running across it from right to left.

Charlie would keep a continuous jumble of logs banging down onto this tray from the large steel forks fitted to the arms of his tractor. As they landed, they were pulled slowly to the left, falling eventually into a V-shaped trough mounted perpendicularly to the tray, with its own dogged chains running toward me, just to my left. As the logs approached I pulled a lever to bring a 25-inch chain-saw bar down on them, just as they came through a sort of guillotine. This was no ordinary chain saw, because it was run along with the rest of the functions from an 80-horsepower diesel engine. It went through huge logs in seconds and dropped the pieces right into yet another wedge-shaped metal trough, this one with an eight-way splitting blade at my end of it.

I pulled another anonymous-looking lever and the wedge shot forward, splitting the log eight even ways. As the blade retreated, the hopper tilted away from me and dumped the pieces onto an elevator that took them up and out of the shed, to drop them in the back of a waiting truck. As these pieces were tipped to the elevator, my eyes shot back to the advancing log, and I cut another piece to split, as I advanced the next.

We split 100 cords one week after work. Just to put the strength of these machines in perspective, some of them send the splitting head forward with 10 tons of force behind it. I witnessed a piece of knotted beech falling into the splitting tray sideways, and before my eye could tell my hand to halt, I had pulled the lever for the split. The blade came forward and cut the piece into a ragged wad, forcing the eight partitions of the wedge through the wood across the grain.

Charlie was a bit old school, or crazy (sometimes a murky distinction), and he would lumber around without earplugs, checking to make sure the case of beer he had put at my feet didn't need refreshing (it didn't), and occasionally clambering down the arms of the tractor with amazing ease, a huge old Husqvarna held in one mitt for the purpose of cutting loose some snag or bent log from the advancing chains. He was a big man, inside and out, could work almost anyone under the table, and is as sorely missed on these pages as in the woods. Luckily his tradition of level-headed and law-abiding workmanship is being carried on by his young son. I was running the machine one day when a small hose on the hydraulics of the front-end loader burst.

Charlie was pissed because he was not going to be able to keep up with me, and the whole workday would grind to a halt when I finished the logs already advancing across the tray.

His son piped up, "I'll go get a new one in Greenfield." This seemed like a nice gesture to me, but Greenfield was 35 minutes away and the tractor supply store would be closing before that. Charlie gave him a strange look and reluctantly said all right. Twenty seconds later a stripped-down street bike with no plates blew out the side door of a low barn and shot a huge rooster tail of dirt from under its fat rear tire as it left the field and squealed out onto the tarmac. The same bike pulled back into the drive about 40 minutes later, just as I was indeed finishing up the logs on the tray. I never thought that an illegal, 120 mph run up the interstate would be an integral part of a day's work on the cordwood, but if you have the technology, why not use it, I suppose. It's your company now, son.

3 TIMBER!

IT HAS BEEN SAID that you can't teach an old dog new tricks. What about the dog that already has some pretty useful tricks? Dad has brought down many more trees than I have at this point, and he has learned the little techniques and subtleties necessary to do this dangerous task efficiently and safely. He will ramble, though, so if it gets too dry skip to the part where he gets eaten alive by hornets.

Good Fellers

The actual felling is the necessary, thrilling, and obviously dangerous part. It should never be attempted if you are tired, angry, or impatient. Of course you should *never* handle a saw (or an ax, a maul, or a hatchet, for that matter) after taking any drug, including alcohol, which does, my children, mean beer. The idea is for the good ole boys to get old. Heed the safety advice in this book, in the saw manufacturer's manual, and in the wisdom of the eldest woodsmen in the village. (Count their fingers before following their advice.)

Felling is a negotiation between where the tree wants to fall and where you want it to land. Take a moment before you begin. Some of us thank the tree first, like saying grace before a meal. Next, scan the upper branches for "widowmakers," dead or dangling branches that your work may suddenly and fatally dislodge. Then determine which way the tree leans. Old master Harry Guyette (see page 71) brings a plumb bob to the woods. He backs off, lets the weight dangle, and sights past it to the tree. Afterward, he circles 90 degrees around the trunk and repeats the procedure, remembering both times to take into account the

1 Make the first of the two notch cuts horizontally, about a third of the way through the trunk. This cut should be on the side of the tree in the direction you wish it to fall.

2 Cut down into the first cut with the second of the notch cuts. The steeper, and deeper, this cut is, the faster the tree will fall.

3 Make sure that the wedge-shaped chunk comes completely free, and that the line at the terminus of the cutout is free of chunks. At the very beginning of a tree's toppling, even a little obstruction can throw it off course.

preponderance of the branches as well as the trunk. This gives him a good indication of which way the tree leans and how heavily. Then he looks in that general direction for a good landing spot (no buildings, power lines, or other trees). Note that Harry takes his time — 93 years old so far and still at it. Felling is something you shouldn't rush into, because once the tree starts to move, it's beyond your control and is extremely powerful.

Everyone "hangs up" an occasional tree (and we'll talk you through your first such screwup), but no one wants to do so more than necessary. It isn't the safest way to put a tree on the ground. If the path isn't clear, you must either abandon your choice for a safer one or fell one or two trees to prepare a path for your tree to fall. The idea is not to play pick-up sticks. It is possible to "swing" a tree a few degrees from where it wants to go toward where you'd like it to fall. More on this later.

Practice in gauging the lean of a tree and making the cuts is obviously crucial. Don't hesitate to look over the tree one more time before you begin. Never be afraid to leave a tree standing if you're not confident that felling it will be safe.

A Notch in Your Trunk

Let's assume that there is a good landing place in the direction that the tree leans. Clear an area about 6 feet around the trunk of brush, fallen branches, snow, and anything else you might trip over. Plan an escape route for yourself. The escape should lead at an angle away from the trunk and the falling path of the tree. I like to head for the nearest big tree and get behind it, when possible.

Once you have attended to these safety measures, you may get to the business at hand. Stand on the side of the tree toward which it will fall. Pick a "target": the spot on which you want the tree to fall, or a more distant landmark in the same line of sight. Draw a mental line from the target to the trunk. This is the point where you cut the notch, which guides the tree's fall. You will use the bottom of the bar for all the cuts in the felling procedure. With your back directly toward the target,

make a cut parallel to the ground and almost a third of the way through the trunk. Next, starting 8 to 10 inches above this first cut, make a second cut angling sharply down so that the two intersect at that spot almost one-third of the way through the trunk. Remove the wedge of wood. This is your guide notch.

Most loggers and competitive lumberjacks insist on clearing every last bit of sawdust from the notch before making the felling cut, to avoid any obstruction that might redirect the falling tree. I've never had this happen, mainly because I always make sure to get the last of the wedge out of there. It takes only a second and if it makes the felling more accurate, then it's more than worth the time.

Wedge When Necessary

A particularly angled tree, or one that you're trying to fell into the wind, may require plastic felling wedges after the felling cut has been started. Drive at least two of them into the felling cut, spaced evenly around the center point of the cut and angled toward the target. Now the tree won't be able to fall back toward you. Just pounding in the wedges may be enough to finish felling the tree. If not, continue cutting, right through the wedges if necessary (that's why they're plastic).

Make the Felling Cut

Go to the other side of the tree. Imagine a line from the target to the notch and on through the trunk. This is where you want to begin the felling cut. This cut should be parallel to the ground and 2 to 3 inches above the level of the bottom of the notch. Cut straight through toward the target. Pause when you've cut most of the way through. When the tree begins to fall depends on its size; thicker trees often begin to fall when there's still an inch or more to go. The piece of wood left is called the "hinge." It helps to guide the trunk as it falls. If you cut all the way through the hinge, unpleasant things happen: You can lose control of the trunk, and it can pinch the saw. Never cut clear through the hinge.

Get Out of the Way

As the tree begins to fall, do the following:

1. Turn off the saw engine.
2. Step back a few strides. The butt of the tree may swing back as it falls or bounce back off the ground with tremendous force.
3. Enjoy the thrill. (One of our projects has been to try to record the sound and the seismographic whoomp a big tree makes. Like us, you probably don't have the right sound equipment, but your heart won't forget it.)

1 Begin cutting horizontally through the back side of the trunk, slightly above the terminus of the felling notch.

2 Saw straight through from the point on the back side of the trunk directly opposite where you want the tree to go, and heading straight toward that point. Do not cut all the way through the trunk, or you're likely to pinch your saw. Leave a "hinge" of a couple of inches to help control the fall of the tree.

Practice in gauging the lean and making the cuts is obviously crucial. Don't hesitate to look it over one more time before you begin. It bears repeating: Never be afraid to leave a tree standing if you're not confident felling it will be safe. I would encourage you to learn on small trees in easy, open environments.

To gain confidence and skill, practice your aim in straightforward felling situations, like a small maple at the edge of an open field. Take an extra minute or two to pick out a specific target, or tap a stick into the ground and try to crush it. By honing your skills when the felling is easy, you'll be better prepared to deal with difficult felling scenarios when they arise.

Tips for First-Timers

➤ Have someone with you, or within close earshot.

➤ Leave the dog in the house. Unless superbly trained, Rover *will* chase that squirrel under the toppling birch and you'll have to replace him before Jimmy gets home from camp.

➤ Don't go felling crazy and leave too many downed trunks jackstrawed at once. It's much harder to buck up that way.

➤ Take a break now and then; too much time with the head down and the ears plugged will lull you into mistakes.

➤ Check the treetops for wind. (The wind at the top matters; the breeze around the trunk does not.) Wind can make a big difference in felling, especially if the branches still have leaves.

3 This tree is going to fall on its own now, if there are no obstructions. It will be a nice, controlled fall, so get back away from it now. Continue cutting for just a second or two longer only if needed (if the tree stops falling).

4 All that's left is to cut the stump flush with the ground and buck up the trunk.

Swinging Butts and Barber Chairs

Strangely, one of the more dangerous trees is the one that leans too much in the right direction. This is because the trunk can "barber chair" before it falls. The heavily leaning tree may begin to fall too fast, breaking the trunk in an unusual fashion. The front of the trunk remains stationary while the bulk peels back, swinging the butt with tremendous force toward you as the tree falls. The resulting stump looks like a barber chair, hence the name. Here's how to fell these trees safely:

After making the notch, extend the bottom or level cut by cutting a 1-inch-deep groove around each side of the trunk to the

1 A tree that has a pronounced lean can be a little tricky. It's a good idea to start by judging where you think it wants to go.

2 The first cut will be a notch that goes no more than a few inches into the trunk, as this old girl doesn't need a lot of help.

back; then begin the felling cut. The grooves will prevent the front side of the trunk from holding fast when the tree begins to fall.

Now for the tree that isn't so cooperative. It is possible to swing a tree approximately 30 degrees from its natural path. After determining where the tree "wants" to go and selecting your target, cut the notch pointing toward where *you* want the tree to land, as usual. The felling cut is where the difference occurs. Begin the felling cut on the side where the tree wants to fall, 3 to 4 inches from the notch. Then cut your way around the back of the tree to the center point and proceed forward, directly toward your target. With practice you can become gratifyingly accurate.

There is a new method of felling being taught by some state forestry services. It involves leaving a "strap" or "trigger" of wood on the back of the tree as you make the felling cut. The last thing you saw through is this strap. The result: You are standing, rather than crouching, and can get farther away, faster. This is a good thing. However, to make a felling cut with a strap or trigger demands making a boring cut, using the nose of the bar. This is a delicate operation, since the nose is near the kickback zone. Therefore it is best learned after you have become adept at the basic method, called "chasing the hinge," which is described in the first few pages of this chapter.

3 Then I'll make a relief cut along both sides of the trunk, leading back from the notch to the spot where I'll make the felling cut.

4 These cuts will help reduce the risk of the dreaded "barber chair" (a trunk that kicks its butt back at you as it falls).

1 Here, I'm making the first cut of a notch on a leaning tree.

2 Once the notch is made, I start on the relief cuts, then move around to the back of the tree to make the felling cut.

3 The remaining fibers in the hinge are put under incredible stress right now and tear from the stretching. I get out of the way.

4 Once the tree falls, it will (ideally) be free from the stump and bang to the ground with a satisfying thump, ready to be bucked up.

The hard plastic felling wedges I mentioned are extremely useful in a pinch (or rather to avoid one). They are strong, yet the saw will cut through them without damaging the chain. Use them in the felling cut anytime you think a bigger tree might fall the wrong way. Pound the wedges securely into the cut, and the tree won't come back that way. When you're swinging a tree, you can pound the wedges in, insert the bar farther into the felling cut, and keep cutting. The tree won't lean back toward you and pinch the blade.

Know When You're Out of Your League

Even straight, beautiful specimens must someday be too old to continue standing safely, and it falls to a man to have to cut one down. The odds of this man being you or me are slim, for sheaves of men like grass have grown and died during the life of a hearty dooryard maple. Nonetheless, it must be done and can be quite tricky. Tree services carry massive insurance policies and charge steep rates because of the very real danger to their climbers and your house. If the tree doesn't have a distinct cant away from the house, and you're not some type of saw-toting squirrel, then you may want to retain the services of these hearty fellows.

If the monster you're plotting against is out of range of your buildings, you have dodged the biggest bullet. Now you need worry only about damage to your saw. Dooryard trees are notoriously laden with foreign bodies. Dad and I have found buried barbed wire, countless sap spouts puckered over with new sapwood, all manner of hooks and nails, and on a few occasions loose constellations of shotgun pellets. Once while working in an old mill I came across a 2 by 6 that had been miraculously cut along the plane of a bullet's burrowing, crescent-shaped path into the soft pine. The fibers of the tree had swirled inward, forming a frozen eddy behind the now comically bent slug.

Spouts, bullets, and pellets are soft metal, but a hank of wire, preserved from rust by the scarring wood, will take the edge off every tooth on the chain before you can pull back. For these reasons we each keep an older, worn-down chain for cutting down such trees. Keep in mind that any really old tree you come across with many branches close to the ground came of age out in the open and may well have been a fence post and a doorman to a family long since descended down the hills and rivers to new yards and younger trees.

All hung up. This tree will be tricky, and a little dangerous, to bring the rest of the way down. I just didn't think those little guys would hold her.

Hang-Ups

I remember a tree that can be instructive for a number of reasons, not the least of which is the cache of new curses it birthed. This was a massive old maple that we dropped directly into a coppice of young shadblow (shad from here out) by mistake. They all bent over away from the butt of the 3½-foot-diameter specimen and halted its earthbound arc 10 degrees from the forest floor. Each of the five troublesome trees was under different pressures and strains. The largest was in the neighborhood of 10 inches across, on down to the youngest brother, a 3-inch problem in the making.

I began by undercutting the former but could proceed no more than an inch before the tremendous weight of the maple pinched the cut shut. I started in from the top, just opposite my undercut, and the victim began to delaminate violently, feathering upward until the side of the cut farthest from the ground looked like a broom. Alternating with little cuts top and bottom, I managed to get safely through this first support, and the huge maple we were after settled 4 or 5 feet closer to its intended landing spot. At this point I realized that the 10-foot "stump" of the shad I had just liberated was going to be in my way. As it was no longer under the influence of the maple, I figured it was fair game and started to simply cut downward through the tree a few feet from its base, to get it out of my way.

How Not to Fell a Tree

Stephen

These instructions make felling trees sound easier than it is. Aside from the inevitable hung-up trees, here are a few felling stories. The worst place I ever dropped a tree was in a briar patch in Georgia, where they grow 'em long and sharp. It was a loblolly pine for pulpwood, so the few branches were way up at the top, which translated to way out in the middle of the briar patch. I should mention that this was more than 30 years ago, in the bad old days before I wore a helmet or ear protection. (Say what?) I backed and elbowed and squirmed painstakingly, literally, through the prickers until I came

to the first limb. I trimmed it and winced my way to the next. As I cut it, I felt a hot pain in my scalp. I thought it must have been a thorn and kept cutting. But then there was another and one in my shoulder. I shut off the saw (my only smart move) and could immediately hear the angry swarm of hornets whose nest I had dropped the tree on. Running through briars while being stung by hornets makes the rock *and* the hard place look pretty comfy.

The worst place I ever saw a tree not dropped was by Frank at a neighbor's house. He'd gone off to work at the neighbor's one day, and an hour later he came roaring back to the house. "Dad, can you help me?"

We went to take a look at the situation. A tree he was supposed to fell had gone all wrong. It had collapsed on the notch cut (probably the notch was cut too deep) and was leaning sickeningly toward the roof. After a brief consultation ("What the hell were you thinking," etc.), we came back with come-alongs, ropes, and felling wedges and were able to pull the tree back the way it was supposed to go.

Note to any neighbors generous enough to have purchased this book: Frank worked for many people in the area, and I'm sure this must have happened at someone else's place. Also, my other son Charlie may become a lawyer. Whew.

After the excitement I was still wondering how my son had gotten into such a mess, when I remembered a double-trunk tree at my old landlord's house, years ago. I had agreed to remove it in lieu of some rent. I went over on a busy day when I really didn't quite have the time. Despite the two stems, I was pretty sure which way the tree wanted to fall and thought I could take a shortcut rather than felling the two stems individually. So, I made a notch in one trunk and was halfway through the felling cut in the other when the damn thing divided in two. It split right down the middle, and one trunk missed the corner of my landlord's roof by just a few inches; the other trunk pinched the bar. That was a long time ago; why, I must have been about Frank's age. The biggest trees eventually fall on their own, and time and memory bring us all down to earth.

We have a friend who tops (crushes? smashes?) all our felling disaster stories. She tells of the time when her family had just bought a farm and decided to remodel an abandoned henhouse into a little guest cottage.

One problem: There was a large dead tree looming over the building. Her dad and a friend sized up the situation, lined up the tree's angle, and eyeballed the henhouse's location. They drew up diagrams, battle plans, and maps. Conclusion: The tree wanted to fall on the henhouse, but the guys wanted it to fall right where "X" marked the spot. More plotting went on, late into the night.

The day of the battle dawned bright and clear. The guys tied a rope to the trunk of the tree and stationed Agent Y at one end of the rope, at an appropriate angle to the proposed path of descent. After one last reconnoiter, Agent Z started the saw. As he made the felling cut, the tree swayed and then, slowly and inevitably, began to lurch toward the henhouse. No problem.

Agent Y tightened his grip on the rope, dug in his heels, and braced himself. As the thousand-pound tree gathered momentum, it dragged poor Agent Y (perhaps 175 pounds) struggling and stuttering across the yard. He lost the tug-of-war, but he was first at the scene of the crime. The trunk had neatly bisected the roof and collapsed the henhouse.

The best-laid plans of many men lie under the wreckage of outbuildings. Oh well; remodeling had begun with a bang.

Remember, the dangers of felling are hard on those who love you. My wife and I have kept alive a practice of some old-timers in the neighborhood. Connie worries when I'm felling and she can often hear the saw, the crash of the falling tree, and then the silence. So I always rev the saw several times afterward, to let her know I'm okay. Who says men can't communicate?

1 After a tree has been downed, the first step is to "limb" it — to cut off any branches to make it easier to get at the trunk and also to eliminate points of contact with the ground. Bucking up a tree with so many pressure points can create a situation where pinching is likely to happen (see page 60). Be sure to feel for branches that may be out of sight but still propping up the trunk.

2 Once the tree is limbed, you can start bucking it up into stove-length pieces. Be careful with your footing if you're working in the snow.

3 When cutting with another sawyer, make sure you're not relieving trunk pressure he's counting on, or creating stresses he's not anticipating.

I learned a lesson at this point, without hurting myself, and whenever that happens while dealing with hung-up trees and chain saws, you can count yourself lucky. There had been so much shearing pressure between the parallel fibers in the shad trunk that they had slipped past one another rather than tearing. As I cut downward through these displaced fibers I unintentionally allowed them to try to return to their previous positions. My saw became as jammed as it ever was, right in the middle of an utterly innocuous stretch of unencumbered wood. It was a strange sight, but that didn't make my bar any less stuck, and I had to take the bar off the saw (really the saw from the bar) so that it didn't hang awkwardly and do more damage. By some careful cutting with another saw, and a few shots with an ax, I was able to free the poor thing and continue on warier, if not wiser. I think you'll find that a fair amount of Yankee wisdom is merely well-placed cynicism.

Buck It Up

Once your tree is safely on the ground, the more mundane but equally tricky task of turning it into firewood begins. You must "limb" the tree and then "buck it up." Limbing should probably be called delimbing, but there we are. The trunk of a tree will often be held up off the ground by a number of limbs and forks. It is safest to buck the trunk into stove-length pieces when it has settled to the ground. Cut

Back atcha. Touching the top side of the end of the bar to a log you're bucking up is a surefire way to get a kickback from the chain saw.

off any branches that you determine to be free of any stresses, that is, branches that are not pinned under the trunk or bent by a neighboring trunk. Let these drop away from the trunk, and then move on to the stressed branches. You have likely just taken a good amount of weight off the tree, as well as removed large branches on the top side of the trunk that might be exerting leverage on the downed tree, making it prone to rolling to one side or the other. The remaining branches need to be handled carefully. There can be a tremendous amount of energy still stored in a tree whose trunk is suspended only a few feet from the ground. Think of it as being in an interrupted state of falling, if that helps.

When trying to determine how to approach a stressed limb, try to imagine where it wants to be, as well as which way gravity is pulling the trunk. Start a tentative cut on the side of the branch *toward which* the end of that branch wants to go. If you were just cutting a limb off a standing tree, you would want to cut up a little way from the bottom, and then start down from the top and meet that

cut. The tricky part is getting your chain free before the cut pinches shut. This is a matter of feel as well as sight.

Keep in mind that a branch being bent forcibly one way will pinch shut much, much faster than one simply affected by gravity. Stressed branches will also shred or snap with very little provocation, so go carefully, with the saw as far from your body as is comfortable. If a branch starts to shred and delaminate quickly at the slightest cut and is *not* a limb holding the trunk off the ground, you can keep scoring it lightly until it falls free or all of its energy is spent. If it is a big branch and you fear it may smack you, then you can leave it overnight and hope it continues to break and slacken on its own. Waiting should not be necessary often.

If you must cut a stressed branch anywhere but at the trunk, always remember to put your body on the side of the cut that is safer. Almost always this is the end of the branch that will be free of the tree, *not* the side still connected. Make a series of small, experimental cuts if you fear pinching.

Buckaroo. Time to buck up the logs into rounds and split them into stove-length pieces.

Pinching and Kickbacks

When bucking up trees by yourself, there are four real dangers, two of which concern your body and two the body of your saw. The two most common dangers to your body are kickbacks from the saw and shifting of the tree. A kickback can occur from the chain being pinched or from improper use of the tip of the bar. When cutting down through a piece of wood, it is important to notice and remember whether the wood is suspended where you're making the cut, or whether it is resting solidly on the ground or on another felled tree. If the tree is suspended, at some point the top of the cut will pinch closed, possibly stalling out your saw and damaging the bar, but certainly costing you time at the least.

Sometimes this pinch can be subtle, and if it just puts a little pressure along the top of the bar, out near the end, the saw will keep running. However, cutting the wood will no longer be the path of least resistance. Instead, the chain will stay stationary for an instant, and the saw will effectively rotate around this spot and jump up in your face. You do not want this to happen. The way to avoid the risk when a trunk is fully off the ground is easy. Simply cut down until you sense the slightest closing, then draw the saw out toward you. Do not try to go vertically back through the cut, as the top is currently narrower than the chain. Then cut upward right toward your first cut; this second cut will open naturally for you as you proceed.

If there is still pinching pressure and you don't have the luxury of a trunk suspended with some room underneath, make a series of cuts as deep as you dare at 16-inch intervals. (Your stove or furnace may be bigger or smaller, but I say 16 inches here just to remind Dad, who confuses *our* stove with the boilers aboard the *Lusitania*.) When you finally get to a place where it is possible to go all the way through, make the cut, then use a peavey or other lever to roll the log to where you can go back and cut down on all the previous cuts.

Freeing a Pinched Saw

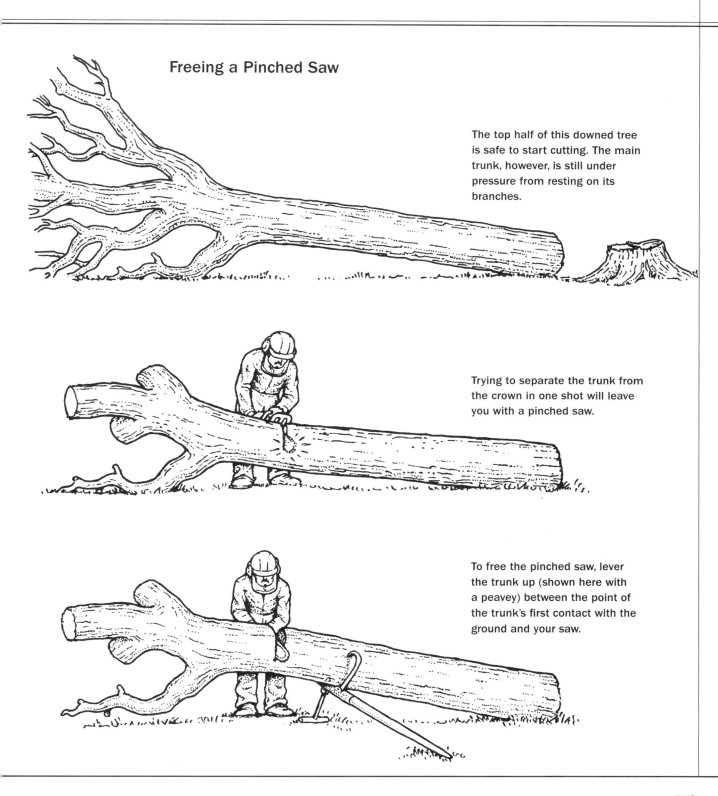

The top half of this downed tree is safe to start cutting. The main trunk, however, is still under pressure from resting on its branches.

Trying to separate the trunk from the crown in one shot will leave you with a pinched saw.

To free the pinched saw, lever the trunk up (shown here with a peavey) between the point of the trunk's first contact with the ground and your saw.

CHOP PSYCHOLOGY

Lincoln Fish is a contemplative man, and it may have been this propensity to think on things that convinced him in high school that he wanted to be a psychologist. He took a test administered him by his guidance counselor, and it came back with the overwhelming certainty that he should be a forester.

Linc lives in a sturdy house built by his grandfather on the southern slope of a wooded hill in western Massachusetts. Here, he cuts and splits four to five cords of ash and red maple each season with his two sons.

He's also an independent private consulting forester, and most of his days are spent acting as the delicate fulcrum between landowners and logging concerns. He walks the land with the specific purposes of the landowner in mind (culling timber, clearing for development, or simply cosmetic management of woods and wetlands). Linc says landowners should get an evaluation from a forester before they head out to the back forty. "The most important thing is to have someone who really knows what they're doing have a look at it. A lot of these old Yankees wander around out there and say, 'Oh, I can log this myself,' and they cut down a tree that is gaining ten to fifteen percent in value every year. Or, they just jump at the logger who says, 'I'll give you ten grand right now for that plot of trees right there,' and then he leaves you with nature's rejects, just spindly and gnarled trees on your land and nothing else." This is truly sound advice, and a tip that any of you heading out to the woods with a saw should take advantage of.

As Linc walks from his dooryard into his own woods, he eyes his trees with thoughts of the future. There is and will be good money in his pine, oak, and cherry down the road. Linc's son is just beginning to run the chain saw, and Linc has come to the same conclusion that I have: "It's just the best therapy there is. The saw is loud, loud, loud, and I know that can be bad for other reasons, but just as a way to go out and rip that cord and let off some tension it is great." Maybe Linc was right about being a psychologist in the first place.

Bodily Harm

The other, more common way kickbacks occur is if you decide to enter Rhode Island politics. No, really, there is a more common way, and that is by touching the end of the top of the bar to any horizontal surface. It is easy not to do this on the primary piece of wood you are cutting, but I have had some close calls by concentrating too much on the cutting going on close to me on the underside of the bar (where the cutting should be taking place) and not the tip of the bar. Often while limbing a tree, you must cut a number of branches or trunks that are parallel and close to one another. If the top of the tip of your bar hits anything, it will run up that surface. Imagine a very fast-moving tank tread. Rather than cutting through the wood, the tip of the bar will act like a car tire going sixty and throw the bar back toward your face and shoulders. Always be aware of the tip of your blade while cutting in close. Never try to cut anything from below with the end of the blade; you are asking for the whole thing to come right back at you, and it *will* be a mess.

Be wary while bucking up trunks and branches, as the second main danger to your body is likely to occur at this stage of the operation. While freeing up sections of the trunk, you will release energy stored in the tree if it is anything but perfectly settled, and things can fly loose in very counterintuitive ways.

Roller derby. Here I'm trying to get a maple trunk up off the ground for cutting.

Logs can spring free and roll your way, so you need to pay close attention to which way is uphill, and put yourself on that side. Check to see whether the trunk fell down along a still-standing tree, as sometimes the mere friction of the butt on the ground is enough to keep a trunk from swinging to one side or the other because of the loaded pressure of another tree farther toward the crown. When you free a section of the butt, the rest may lurch quickly to one side.

A Pain in the Saw

Less serious than bodily harm, but potentially as time consuming, is damage to your saw. The forces involved in limbing and bucking up a tree are not as great as those in fell-ing, but they are less straightforward, and the pure number of opportunities for things to go wrong makes this stage tough on your saw. Probably the most common mistake during bucking is touching the tip of the chain to the ground. Even the softest loam has little pebbles and the like, which will dull a chain faster than you might think. This can happen in an instant as you are trying to get through that last 1 or 2 inches to free up a round from the trunk. It is worth almost any amount of peavey work to roll logs and cut the last bit from above rather than risk dulling a chain. Sometimes in bucking up a tree that has been felled for some time, you'll roll it over and find dirt frozen to the trunk in a long stripe where it was touching the ground. I have always

Jackstraw! A winter's worth of warmth. Cut as much as you can while the logs are propped in the air, but be careful of shifting.

Taping Timber

Frank

I distinctly recall the first time I heard my father bellow a word everyone understands and children find particularly exciting. It's not the same word he bellowed when a cylinder head in the Dodge let go, or the choice morsels heard by Skylab that he let fall upon seeing the hand-chamfer job I did on the new woodwork in the kitchen.

No, as some long since vaporized hardwood creaked and prepared for the inevitable, he killed the saw and let rip with "Timber!" He did not draw it out, as he would years later when we started felling together, and some levity was all right. He is the loudest yeller I know (his sneezes can be heard above the classic farm procession of a tractor, a baler, and a wagon, while in full swing). Dad is remarkably no-nonsense when it comes to trees falling on his sons, and he may well have reserved his loudest whoops for moments of kinetic opportunity: equipment firing up, rams let loose in the sheep pasture, shell levered into rifle chamber. All this was ahead of me at that point, and his yell, though I had been forewarned about it, caught me off guard and made me feel like a bucker in some remote timber camp in northern Maine. I was so caught up in how cool the whoop had been that I had to wait till he felled another maple to really appreciate the creak-to-whoosh-to-thud procession that has given me so much satisfaction ever since.

One snowy winter we tried to record this very gallimaufry of sound. My brother gave me a small recorder and I brought it out to the woods with us. The results we got were disappointing. The most satisfying part of a good clean toppling job is the heavy bass thump when the trunk of the tree about three-quarters of the way up hits ground. It seems to be this portion of the tree, at any rate. I think it is because this is the spot moving the fastest that still has some real meat to it, still unbroken by too many branches. In any event, the little recorder was not up to the task of reining in the enormity of the sound. We later realized that we had hamstrung the poor thing, in a way, by not putting it on the ground. It had been hanging from a small branch on a wisp of a sapling and couldn't sense the thud. I don't know what good a faithful recording would do anyhow, but if I had one I'm pretty sure I could get good use from it. Maybe anytime someone tells a really bad joke, I could press the button in my pocket and let them know my feelings with a withering digital rendition of nature's clunker.

Roundabout. A summer gust whips the sawdust from a round of newly cut maple.

Avoid touching the tip of the running saw to the ground. Small stones and soil will quickly dull the chain.

taken the time to chip it free, just in one little spot, every 16 inches to avoid unnecessary chain touch-ups.

The other, more serious but less likely damage to your saw while limbing and bucking is pinching the blade. Sometimes there is unpredictable energy stored in the tree, and the wood will squeeze in an unforeseeable way, and your bar will become wedged. More often, in my experience, a person will be rushing and try to go too deep from the pinching side of the cut, and not be able to back out in time. If the bar is not pinched too ferociously, you can pound a splitting, felling, or improvised wedge into the top of the cut and take the pressure off enough to pull the bar free. Sometimes this is not enough, and you will need to figure a way to heave upward on the offending log from the point directly below the trapped saw.

If a saw is pinched this badly, you must check the chain and the groove in the bar before firing back up. Make sure the saw is *off*. If the pinch stalled out the saw, you may not have turned it off, and the check you must perform requires turning the engine over manually. After making sure the saw is turned off at the switch, gently pull the chain along the bar for at least one full circuit. If it runs smoothly, fire back up and get back to work. If not, you have to find the spot along the groove where the chain is catching. Then slacken the chain enough to free it from the bar, and very, very gently and painstakingly use a flathead screwdriver (you should have one out there with you, along with whatever other driver your saw may take) to pry the sides of the groove back to their parallel state. This may produce little dings and burrs; you can smooth these by running the screwdriver back and forth with some force, or you can use a very fine file if things are really ugly. At this point you should also run the chain through your hands a few times, bending each link to the next, to make sure they didn't get pinched into some kind of stiffness that will keep the chain from whipping smoothly around the end of the bar or sprocket.

The Yearly Cycle of Bucking and Felling

Here is an **ideal schedule** for producing dry, high-quality cordwood.

Late Fall

Fell trees for next year. Buck. Split. Pile or stack. Cover. (Don't use plastic, as it sweats like crazy on sunny days and doesn't allow for drying. Sheets of corrugated metal are an easy alternative.) Allow to season through following winter, spring, and summer.

Early Fall of Next Year

Stack the wood in the shed. Burn. Repeat.

Now, news from the **real world**, where many accommodations are made between the ideal and the possible. Here's what we really do.

Late Fall and Winter

Fell trees for next year. Limb. Leave them.

Early Spring

Drag limbed trees out of woods with tractor. Pile them (with tractor) in a sunny place.

Spring and Summer

Buck the trunks. Split.

Early Fall of Next Year

Stack the wood in the shed.

Late Fall and Winter

Fell trees for the following year. Limb. Leave them. Go in by the stove.

If you get the wood felled and limbed all at once, you can break up the rest of the work over weekends and evenings.

A Basic Schedule

The advantages of any schedule for firewood are idiosyncratic. It has to work for you and your equipment in such a way that you don't handle the wood *too* many more times than is necessary. We like the real-world schedule shown on page 61 because we make sparing use of a tractor (one day). Also, we don't litter the forest with 16-inch pieces of cordwood that we later have to try to find under cover of snow, spring ferns, summer briars, clouds of mosquitoes, and so on. The wood is in the sun and the breeze all spring and summer, so it is lighter and easier when we split it, carry it, and stack it. Purists might point out that if it were split the previous fall, it would

dry better. For us, it would be drying in the shade of the woods. This way, it is split and then promptly stacked in an airy shed, which works wonders.

You will devise your own schedule. Whether you do the whole process yourself or buy log lengths or stove-length split wood, there is one commandment: The wood must be at least a year old. About half the weight of green wood is water, and it takes a lot of energy to boil it away in your stove. Green wood is hard to light and doesn't throw as much heat as dry, or seasoned, wood.

An old-timer we know, sort of a hilltown Faust, tried to cheat the natural laws of transpiration and aging. He would fell trees in the spring of the year in which they'd be burned. His trick was *not* to limb them right away, but to leave the felled tree on the ground until the leaves opened and, eventually, died. Then he'd limb, buck, split, and sell the 5-month-old firewood that fall as "seasoned." His theory: The leaves would draw all the moisture from the trunk and limbs as they opened and tried to grow. A random sampling of his customers rated his results as "fair." Our advice: Some things take time. It takes the universe about a year to dry firewood and 86 years to bring the Red Sox a world championship. Stop whinin'.

Around the bend. The trunk of a tree we felled (see page 46) had a dogleg that, curiously, landed neatly around this old stump.

Old-Time Tools

Before the days of chain saws and skidders, lumberjacks tromped into the woods with axes and saws to take down big timber. With a sharp double-bit ax and a two-man saw, a logging team could bring down anything from a 100-year-old maple to a 500-year-old giant sequoia.

At the end of the day, a logger in Oregon makes his way home, carefully balancing the blade of a crosscut saw in one hand and gin poles in the other.

Lumberjacks in Minnesota move logs into the river using peaveys.

A woodsman in Oregon uses a double-bit ax to make a felling notch.

The same woodsman and his partner use the crosscut saw to fell this sugar pine.

A scaler uses his "cheat stick" to measure a log.

Two lumberjacks buck up a trunk, the old-fashioned way.

4 SPLITTING & STACKING

ONCE THE TREE has been limbed and bucked up, the woods quiet down, you can untense your arms, and you can kill the saw. It's now that I always notice how much I have been sweating, and how hard the blood is pounding in my ears. Let the noise go away from you, and feel yourself drop back a hundred years. Pick up your maul and start swinging. Split until you tire, then stack for a bit. If you split the wood green, that is, just after felling, it will dry much faster than it would in rounds or as a whole trunk.

Splitting

Somehow, I'll try to explain my love for splitting wood — a task that has made so many so miserable. For one, I find that my best thinking and most productive talking are done while working at something repetitive but variable. There is a moment of silence, sometimes a long moment, while the body gets settled in a rhythm and learns of the particular wood the hands are up against. This done, if I'm with Dad, the talking begins.

We start in, often about baseball, or if either of us has recently seen him, my brother Tood. Dad reads a lot but doesn't see much in the way of television, so he'll often ask what this guy's changeup looks like, or if so-and-so really has doubled in size from being on the juice. Things like this will lead the conversation on a merry moral chase and branch and dart to all subjects, so that by the end of the afternoon the air is like a busy winter clearing, with 10 types of tracks coming and going in a profusion that causes the eye to wonder which sets of prints are transient and which have been coming and going in a daily chase.

One year (it was an election year I'd guess) we developed a political game around throwing split wood. Any piece requiring more than a few shots to split was instantly a candidate, and as long as he lasted on the stump, as it were, we would work up a back story and a platform for him. Upon being split, the pieces were thrown atop a heap 30 feet distant, the pinnacle of which was the dictatorship, or presidency (these should clearly never be confused, but have you read a paper recently?). Sometimes a lucky stick would stay in power for 10 minutes before being violently deposed by a well-aimed, maple-flavored coup. I refuse to list the myriad execrable puns engendered by this game, as you already suffered through the stump gag, though "this guy and his wife split on the maul" wasn't at all bad.

I've never mentioned it in so many words, but these working talks are sometimes Dad's sermons to me, as I can't often be pinned in church. Anything that needs to be said is labored out stroke on stroke, and the wells that fill in our absence are bucketed dry as the newly exposed wood piles up.

"I'll try to explain my love for splitting wood — a task that has made so many so miserable."

Maybe some of you underwent your first oedipal triumph while shooting hoops, flipping the pigskin, or even shooting pool, but my first sickly, overanticipated, and reviled moment in the brutish passing lane of physical development came during a woodpile session. Dad had pretty much turned an old maple round into a broom and decided that it was destined for the fireplace; it was just too tough to split. Dad tossed the thing aside like a Popsicle stick, only to find that I thought it could use one more lick. It may have been a few shots later, but that round did yield to my maul, and another chapter in the "I loosened it for you" canon was written.

Splitting wood may well be the final frontier in the war between my perception and the reality of my father's strength. Honestly, to this day he can still grind me pretty fine over the course of a long day in the sun or cold. Each time I straighten up to wipe my brow in a delicate celebration of a long haul with two huge rounds, he can be seen in the background, unceremoniously completing his third trip with two pieces of the same trunk. It's reassuring to know that a strong stubborn streak can help to crowd out any common sense that might be gained through a life of hard work.

Milquetoast and Ugly Mothers

Frank

It was during a long session in which the two of us were pitted against a gnarled maple (at an age when a boy is still too young to really split and thinks his father is a superhero) that we developed a ranking system for pieces of wood. There was a halfhearted attempt to start with easy pieces, with names like "wussburger," "milquetoast," and so on. For some reason these never stuck, possibly because there are (hopefully) far too many easy pieces.

It was when we started in on a hierarchy of names for the knottiest, crotchetiest, damnedest pieces of wood that things got interesting. It was never actually worked out completely, but it was agreed that "rough customers" and "tough customers" were bad, "ugly mothers" were slightly worse, and "PhDs" were the worst of all. We bantered back and forth, me hopping around, contributing to the fledgling lexicon with such impassioned entries as: "Is that a rough customer, Dad?

You gonna split that in one or two shots, Dad? Is it a rough customer or a tough customer, Dad? Cause it looks rough and tough, right Dad? Dad! You gonna split that rough customer now, Dad?" In retrospect, I probably hadn't made up for all the time I wasted as a little boy until I was about 18. A wonderful and sarcastic farmer from down the road once told my father that when it came to helping out on a farm, "One boy's a boy, two boys is half a boy, and three boys is no boy at all."

wussburger

ugly mother

PhD

Greenhorns and Green Wood

For the people I've introduced to splitting wood, it was the first time in many of their lives that they hit something as hard as they could. Even hitting a baseball seems cleaner and more controlled, maybe because you're sure that the hands and bat will continue more or less unobstructed to the end of the swing. This too is the goal when splitting wood, but you never know where the maul will stop, or how abruptly. There is also much more force at play with a maul. Because of the energy-focusing properties of the blade, much more power is delivered to one spot than with even a sledgehammer. Greenhorns watching an old hand are often taken aback by the violence of the exploding pieces.

Unless I am positive of a piece's easy yield, I swing as if the wood were riddled with knots. There is no more frustrating feeling than knowing you babied a piece that could easily have been split with a stout swing but instead must be sheepishly revisited. As a result of this philosophy, straightforward bolts of wood often receive far more pounds-per-square-inch force than they need, and the resulting halves go whirling and bounding end over end in opposite directions. In unfrozen conditions, the maul often bites deep into the ground at the end of a swing like this, and sometimes

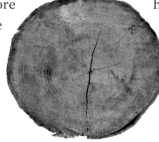

Wise crack. This round is a no-brainer for the maul.

there are sparks and chips of stone. All this to say, splitting wood can seem like a dangerous family of excessive forces and movements to those who have never lashed out with all of their grown strength.

Of the dozen or so people I have shepherded through their virgin licks with a maul, athletes without abandon, like my friend Jim, have picked it up the fastest. Jim weighed well over 200 pounds in college, with broad shoulders and a gusto for new things that often leaves him battered and stitched when he heads back to the city. He picked up both the power and the subtleties of the ancient, proper movements in 10 minutes and would have happily halved half the world, if not for the coming of nightfall.

Anyone with a healthy body and strong hands can do the work in a woodlot, albeit different people will accomplish it at different speeds. Hands really do make the difference. They will be cramped after a long day and sore the next. They will blister up the first few weeks of the new season and hold twin rows of hard calluses for months after the last piece is split and stacked.

No matter how big and strong a person is, the hands are still the last link in the chain of motion that delivers the maul to the wood. When I can't seem to bust a piece I feel I should, it is

Smashing success. Take extra care when splitting a round of wood in the dead of winter — the frozen sap within can cause the wood to snap forcefully apart when the maul comes crashing down.

Split That Tough Customer!

Now then, as a nonacquaintance used to say, "Let's take a rest and split and stack." The felling and bucking up will take some time, but if you choose to do the right thing and split the wood by hand, it'll take more than twice that time. And if, as our swampiest of Yankee forebears, you eschew the mechanized stacker, then it's going to take even longer, friend. (There is no such thing as a mechanized stacker, but you *will* end up desperately trying to invent one in your head while the numbing pieces pile up.)

Some who are sticks in the mud wish to upend each piece of wood at the outset and stick it in the mud. I tend to stand the pieces up as I go, because often the piece just split will tip those nearby as it flies to flinders. One should find a good flat piece of ground, assuming it is all frozen, and an evenly cut, thick piece of wood with knots if the ground is going to yield too much. We often intentionally cut one shorter piece from the stump of the felled tree, or leave the stump level, as a chopping block. This term may have given rise to the woodsman's least favorite semantic mistake. I refer to the term "chopping wood," as it is very often used to describe the act of splitting wood. Almost no one actually chops down trees with axes anymore (and even back in the day, axes were used only for making the felling notch), though a good many do continue to split their own wood with mauls.

often because my hands are going soft at the moment of impact. When I focus on this, on really clenching and snapping my wrists on contact with the wood, I get an extra boost of power. I have often come home from college, hauling brand-new gym muscles out to the woodlot, only to flag long before Dad puts down his maul. There is no substitute for hard labor, and when a good rhythm is achieved, you can split wood all day long. I used to flail away at all the splitting I could, but eventually I realized that bending over to gather split wood and stacking it, or throwing it in a pile, gives the splitting muscles a chance to rest and stretch. Henry Ford would never agree, but breaking up the task while still moving forward will get you more work done by the end of the day.

ONE GOOD STACK

Harry Guyette is 93 and getting his firewood in for about the eightieth time. He is a strange mix of unabashedly practical. He and his brother used to go down to a nearby mill in their truck and bring home cords and cords of sawmill scraps. He wears a thick velcroed back brace over his clothing when it could easily go under his work shirt. He does not want any help with the firewood and scoffs at the idea that his arrow-straight woodpiles come to be through the use of plumb lines or spirit levels.

Harry uses old language and beautifully trimmed turns of phrase. When he's cutting down a tree, he's "falling the thing." Once it had been falled, his brother Merril "drawed the tree out" of the forest with chains on the tractor. If something happens frequently, then it happens "as a rule." He'd say, "As a rule, trees by the road are full of road dust and will take the edge out of your saw pretty quick." Not to mention sap spouts and barbed wire, I thought, but he was already there: "Also lots of things you can't see or predict, but you know it when you've found one."

Dad and I were trying to steer the conversation toward Harry's fabulous woodpiles when we could, and eventually things came round that way. I asked whether he stretched out strings to make the front of the pile so straight. "No, me 'n' Merril just made sure to lay out the stringers straight and put no curves in the stacking." Fair enough, but the faces of these piles are impossibly flat. There was an answer to this too, and it revealed how well matched as workers he and his brother had been: "Merril didn't like to run the saw, so he would mark the trees out at sixteens and I'd cut them up while he drawed out the next one."

Harry spoke of the way people up on his hill used to help each other out: "Once, a man up the road took sick and couldn't get his wood in one fall, so we got a bee up and finished it with some others. My brother and I were the youngest there, and people couldn't believe we didn't think anything of cutting up two-foot beech with the two-man saw. When that was sharp, it would go right through some wood."

Two Ways to Wield a Maul

The overhead explosion. Bringing the maul down from overhead uses a lot of power from the upper back.

The sideways slam. Hefting the maul up from the side involves more torque, somewhat like throwing a baseball.

Study the Victim

When the piece intended for cleaving has been placed on a suitable surface, you should make a quick study of its cut face. Is there a crack running as a radius to the rings? If so, drive that maul right into the crack as long as the wood is small enough to go in your stove as two pieces. If the piece needs to be split into four or more pieces to fit in the firebox, drive the maul into the piece out at the edge, where you estimate the crack's terminus to be, and work your way across, hitting the same seam one blade width closer to the center. This will ideally give you two rough halves, which will each be much easier to split than the original.

Are there any large knots close to what is now the top of the piece? If so, flip it and study again, as it is far easier to get a split started at the end away from the knots. If the stick in front of you is a little too big to be useful in halves, but not really worth busting into quarters, there is a simple solution: Hit it off center, and take off a little half-moon piece. Spin the wood 90 degrees (or move your body to the same angle), and split the remaining piece right down the middle. This may seem like advice too simple to bother giving, but when in the mindset of halving everything, sometimes people forget that rendering a piece of wood into thirds is easy enough and saves a ton of time if quarters are not necessary.

1 Large pieces like this huge round of maple are often easier to split by "peeling" — working your way around the edges, then splitting down the middle

2 Start by taking your first few pieces from around the edges.

splitting

If you want to get really tricky, anytime you clip a piece of wood but don't quite split it all the way, rotate it 90 degrees, and try to hit the center of the split perpendicularly, so that half of the blade of the maul is biting into the far side of the wood and half into the near side. With practice, you can get four pieces in two shots. Keep in mind that the lighter, more fragile two-piece mauls with the flared blades are better for this, as their blades are much taller than the abbreviated, one-piece, square-bladed mauls we use. The only trouble is, they snap if you overshoot that near side of the crack, whereas the metal maul will send a Looney-Tunes vibrating message up the handle and down through your spine.

Big Fellas

If the customer on the block in front of you is so big — anything over 16 inches in diameter — that it will need to be broken down into eight or a dozen pieces, the best approach may be to "peel" the piece. If you can't get that satisfying, hollow boom that indicates a split coming after two or three shots, you may have to employ this strategy. Peeling is a technique in which your first few hits are parallel to an imaginary diameter, but out near the edge rather than in the usual pie-cutting pattern. Work your way around the piece, making it into something like an octagon, or decagon, or sofargon that you don't know what it is. (If you hated that joke, it was Dad's.)

3 When the edges are all split off, start in on the inner sections.

4 It's all over but the cryin', now. Oh, yeah, and the stacking.

This done, you will have a smaller piece with points around its perimeter. Imagine each point as two sides of a triangle, the third side of which you will make with the blade of the maul. You can now easily knock these points off, leaving you with a much more familiar-size piece that can be attacked in the familiar way. Dad calls this "reading" the wood, but so as not to be elitist toward those who split a lot of wood but are listening to this on tape or wish their preliterate children to split more wood, I will call it divination.

Some people like to use splitting wedges on larger pieces, and while I'll admit that these tools have their place, I've never had any trouble, and have saved a lot of time without them. A splitting wedge looks quite a bit like the head of a maul, and indeed I have used an old maul head for a wedge in a pinch. Wedges are heavy and very durable. However, a wedge is designed to be a bit softer than the head of a maul, simply so it will mushroom out of shape rather than chip the striking surface of the maul. If you are going to use wedges, the two-piece, lighter maul is much better suited for pounding them. The one-piece maul, while heavier, features a handle fused to the very back of the head, whereas the two-piece maul has the handle joined about two-thirds of the way from the blade to the poll. This is far more conducive to good hammering.

My main objection to using wedges is speed. You must take at least two or three little whacks at the wedge while holding it to get it set in the wood. Then, too often for my taste, the wedge becomes stuck in a stubborn piece and must be either abandoned or rescued delicately by maul or, even more riskily, by chain saw. Just too much time and energy wasted on a wedge, folks.

Getting a foothold. Wedges are a necessary evil as long as there are knots in the round you're trying to split.

All Dried Up

A note here about the condition of the wood you're splitting, and why to split it up in the first place. If you're cutting a tree of any real size, the pieces it will yield, while ideally fine in length, will be too large in diameter. Breaking these fellas down to size is the obvious reason for splitting cordwood. Another equally compelling reason is to dry the wood. The bark on a felled tree retains water quite well, so the more you can raise the ratio of exposed wood to bark, the faster the wood will dry.

We have found that in a very cold winter it is often faster to split fresh, or green, wood than it is to split wood that has been bucked up and drying for months. The reason is the very moisture we are all trying so hard to get rid of. In a very cold winter the sap in felled hardwoods freezes, and the pieces practically explode when hit. Often traditionally tough wood, like beech with its stringy structure, will split more readily while frozen green. The other advantage is increased drying time, for as soon as the sun gets at these pieces in the spring, they begin to air out while their as yet unsplit brethren may wait for the fall to be opened up.

Bringing in the Wood

There was a fall day sometime in the 1980s when Dad and my brother and I were getting in some wood. We were living in a big old farmhouse typical of New England in

A head start. Particularly tough customers can be started with a vertical chain-saw cut.

its rambling construction, almost like a collapsing telescope or a Russian nesting doll tipped roughly on its side. There were four roofs of decreasing height stacked down and away from the main pitch. The second capped the kitchen, the third the woodshed, and the fourth the garage. In retrospect, this shows me the premium that builders used to place on having firewood to hand rather than a vehicle or a horse, as well as an obvious attitude that said: "Keep the kitchen warm and to hell with the other rooms; we can always store meat and ice in those."

At any rate, it was a cold day, and Dad had long since taught us that work sometimes had to be done in the cold, and that by moving fast we could combat the bitterness that stiffens fingers and senses of humor. We made some variety of game out of filling the wood room and were thrumming along as three-in-one, bending, lifting, tossing. The truck we had at the time had a cap on it nearly year-round for hauling sheep under cover. As Tood and I were so much smaller than Dad, we could almost stand in the bed and were spending our time shoving the wood out so that it could be tossed through the gaping woodshed door. The occasional toss would come up short, but the builders of the woodshed had thought of this. The sill of the broad, tall opening was a ragged old 6 by 6, chewed to curling rafts of splinters all along its corroded surface. It was like an extreme close-up of desert wind erosion, split lengths of maple slowly forcing the sill into the least obtrusive profile by means of thousands of nicks and gouges. Tood and I became so excited by tossing pieces that would (success) or would not (louder, less productive success) clear the sill and fill the wood room.

Sometimes when the components of an engine become overheated, they misfire and break. I rose as Tood ducked to retrieve

The family that stacks together. The saw wasn't running, but my mouth still was. Charlie (aka "Tood") keeps the helmet on while splitting and I stack 'em up.

another piece to hurl, I threw and ducked as he rose to throw, faster and faster. Then, perhaps because one of us let a piece slip from our hands and had to awkwardly dip down again to retrieve it, I rose a fraction after he rose, and caught a round of some forgotten wood on the crown of my head. I had never yet cut my head badly and was astonished and frightened at the amount of blood, and how quickly it left my body. Dad rushed me into the house to evaluate the damage, and in an odd moment of clarity the likes of which one finds only in the shock of an injury, or the calm of impending pressure, I was intensely sorry that I was dripping on the floor my grandmother was washing. I apologized, and she gave me a worried look. Since that day, and that divot in my scalp, the dinged-up sill that marked the line between the very real cold of the outdoors and the soon-to-be-vanquished cold of the wood room and its Btu payload has reminded me of clarity in the cold and sorrow for the wrong things.

There is more in that old wood room than the similarity between the doorsill and my head. That's not even unique, as my head has been compared to all manner of inert hardware. That wood room has a kind of timelessness to it. For a number of reasons, the space between those walls was on a different schedule, a different level of importance, than the rest of the house. We lavished labor on that one room for a few weeks every season and

Ray Gage

There was an old-timer in our town named Ray Gage who taught me a number of things, none of them good and few of them true. He was a deranged-looking old hillbilly, never far from a very intimidating dog he called Cody (among other things). In retrospect this dog could not possibly be as big as he appeared to me as a boy, but I can say with confidence that he was no more than 5 feet tall at the shoulder, and not much over 400 pounds after eating. His smell was bigger, and his coat was an odd, bleached white that had stained yellow for some undoubtedly disgusting reason. Ray used to lam Cody with his cane (he was also the type of guy who makes it all right for me to use the word "lam").

Eventually, Ray would always come around to the following tale from his childhood as an adopted boy in the hills. His new father took him out to the dooryard his first day at his new home and told him to split the pile of wood before him. Then, with a benevolent pat on the shoulder, his new father told him to simply make another pile of any pieces too difficult to split by hand. Having finished, little Ray asked innocently what he was to do next. "Now split the other pile," was the reply.

then carted away its precious store armload by stumbling early-morning armload. The warmer months saw the wood room isolated and utterly ignored.

So there you have it, the wood room spent most of its existence being ignored, and the juicy remainder as a dark, important, and seasonal player in our household drama.

Master and youngblood.
Take note of Harry Guyette's masterpiece (top), as compared to my ragged woodpile (bottom).

The floor of the wood room had never been seen by any of us, as it was always at least a foot deep in the curled rinds of maple, ash, and cherry. Oddly shaped or unusually heavy pieces were perpetually left behind, so that the room developed a kind of prison-colony feel with its perennial ugly, threatening, or useless refugees.

Stacking

If you were to drive down any country road late in the New England fall and ask the first 10 people you came across how to stack wood, you would come away with 10 different methods, as well as reason enough not to use any of them. To my eyes, the only goals when stacking wood are to allow it to dry and not have it fall over. If you can stack it on a porch or in a basement, then walls and posts will be your friends. If it needs to be stacked in the woods for a while, try to find some pairs of sufficiently strong trees for use as bookends for the piles. Any trick variations you may have seen have been engineered either for style or because of a lack of preexisting supports. I will not stoop to speak to the first reason, as a well-stacked pile speaks for itself with elegance and utility.

Stringers and Cribbing

Occasionally some poor soul will find himself or herself in the predicament of having to stack firewood away from any posts, walls, or trees, on ground that is either too frozen or too rocky to drive in good stakes. If this is indeed your predicament, do three simple things. First, lay two long, straight branches (or 2- to 3-inch-thick saplings) parallel to one another and no farther apart than the firewood is long. We'll call these pieces "stringers" from here out, and their purpose in life is to keep the woodpile up off the ground. If space and material permit, you may find it convenient to cut your stringers to 8-foot lengths, so that three 4-foot-tall piles will signal that you have a cord.

The flatter the site for this operation, the better, but if you must be on sloping ground, lay the stringers perpendicularly to the slope of the hill. Then simply shim the lower one, or find stringers of sufficiently different diameters that the two lie both parallel and on the same plane. It isn't crucial to the integrity of the pile that the first row of cordwood be off the ground, but if it's not, you will lose that first layer to rot. Once you have level stringers established, put down your first row of wood, taking care to arrange the pieces as close together, and as close to parallel, as possible.

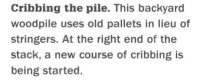

Cribbing the pile. This backyard woodpile uses old pallets in lieu of stringers. At the right end of the stack, a new course of cribbing is being started.

(Remember that if you're stacking on snow, no matter how hardpacked, it will melt and shift. Dad and I have had many a pile tip into the snow and wet ground because we didn't shore them up sufficiently against the ravages of melting.)

Now is the time for the second important item in the construction of a good pile. The second row is where the freestanding pile requires a bit of skill, or at least practice. You need to begin a process called "cribbing," which consists of turning the first two pieces of wood at each end of a new row so that they lie perpendicular to those underneath and out toward their ends (close to flush with the front and back of the pile). Cribbing produces a crosshatched structure similar to a crude log cabin at each end of the pile. These towers, if built from the right pieces, will be enough to support the pile on its own. A good trick is to set aside straight, cleanly split pieces as you stack, so that there is always uniform stock available for cribbing.

The third important point is the simplest and easiest. As you stack, feel free to toss aside all lopsided, wedge-shaped, or just plain ugly pieces of firewood. When these are the only pieces remaining, simply put them on the top of the pile, bark side up, and go on into the house. This top layer is the roof of the pile, and unless the wood is to be taken in and burned directly from this freestanding pile, the bark of the final layer is really all you'll need to protect the pile. If wood must be taken and burned from this pile throughout winter, then a more permanent roof should be used. An old tarpaulin without too many holes or some corrugated sheet metal should do fine.

In the round. Old Man Cooney's gourmet cordwood chimneys take the art of stacking wood in a whole new direction.

Woodpiles around the World

In the Swiss Alps, wood stacking becomes an art form.

Stacks of firewood outside a Russian Orthodox convent in eastern Estonia.

Wood stacked in a traditional Slovenian hay shed.

Don't try to make a call from this phone booth in Scotland . . .

Building a Simple Woodshed

Attached Years before either of us had any professional carpentry experience to our names, we put up a woodshed at our place, and that means you can do it too. We simply found and marked the locations of the studs in the end wall of the kitchen and nailed up a 2-by-6 ledger (**1**). If you want to make things look nice and avoid rot, strip the wall free of a few clapboards, put a piece of flashing as long as your 2 by 6 behind the lowest remaining clapboard and over the top of your ledger, and nail it all in place. Pick an angle shallow enough to shed snow while still allowing enough space to stack wood, and cut 2-by-6 rafters to this angle. Cut enough to provide for one every 16 inches over the length of the ledger. The low end of the rafters can land on a doubled 2 by 6 running on edge between sturdy posts (**2**). Lay sheet metal over the rafters (**3**). Now you have a place for firewood, if not a Rockefeller wedding reception (which are held only in the *finest* of woodsheds).

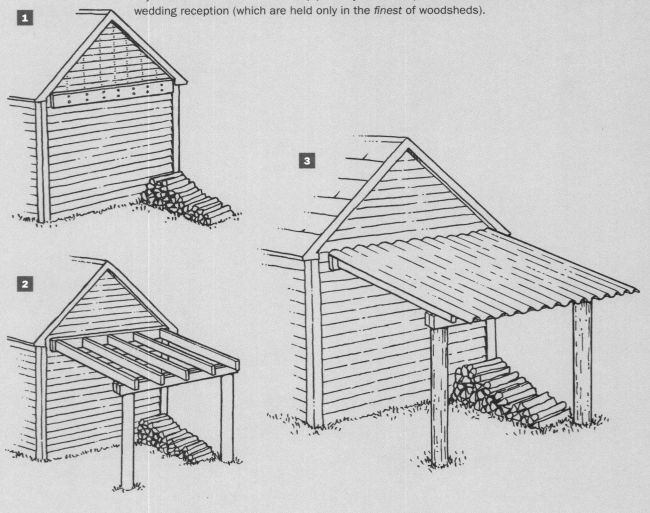

Detached

For those with some building experience who want a woodshed that's separate from the house, we offer plans for this freestanding shed. The base can be either poured concrete or simple wooden pallets with poured footings for the posts (**1**). It's important for the roof to be at least slightly pitched to shed rain and snow. The top of the wall can be left open to increase air circulation (**2**). The finished shed measures 8 feet by 16 feet and will hold up to four cords of wood (**3**).

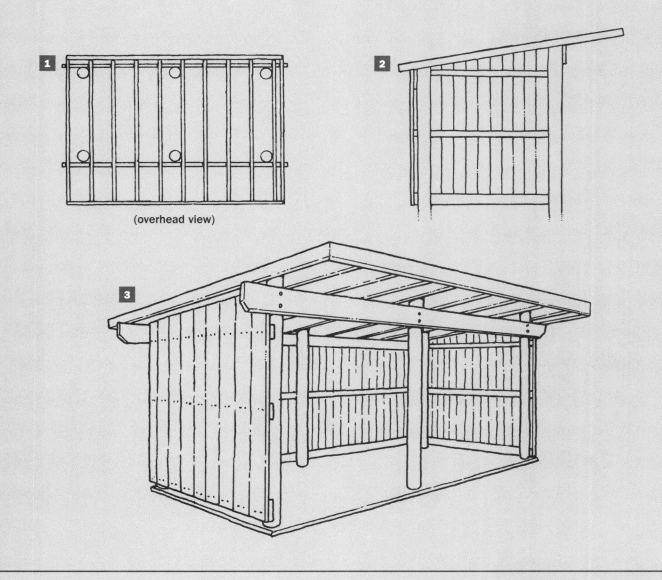

(overhead view)

Low profile. The simple canvas wood hauler is just one step up from the crooked arm.

Free wheelin'. A friend of ours uses this wheeled cart to move wood from the barn to the house. Just don't try pushing a full load down a muddy path.

Top of the line. Although you could probably ride this wood dumbwaiter down to load it up, I wouldn't recommend it.

Cheap labor. If no other implement is at hand, there's always the strong back of (not so) willing offspring.

Other Stacking Methods

I once lived in a little cabin on the eastern slope of a hill in the Berkshires. It was where I had my first stove that was all my own. My landlord was a precise fellow about nearly everything, and his woodpiles were no exception. In fact, he may have been more careful of them than anything else. He stacked wood in a hollow beehive shape he had observed in Scandinavia. Each pile was around 9 feet in height and 6 or 7 in diameter at the base. He called them "wood chimneys," as the idea is for the shape to draw air in, up, and out on sunny days. His wood was always quite dry, so I can't refute the idea. He would just start stacking in a circle, with the fatter end of each piece of wood to the outside. Each row would be laid slightly closer to the center, and by 8 to 10 feet up the whole thing would lean in on itself. One caveat: These invariably turn into the world's swankiest chipmunk condos.

I have also seen people who stack all of their wood in a huge cube. The wood is still in rows, but the rows run tight against each other as deep as they are long. If you don't have the space, or don't want to walk the extra distance to retrieve wood in rows, this is fine. However, like the aforementioned chipmunk condos, a pile with that much depth and protection from the elements and predators is an attractive home for all types of animals. In addition, you'll be displacing these rodents all winter as you move through the pile.

Hilltown Thievery

Now that you've put it all up, keep a watchful eye on your wood, as the longer a bad winter stretches, the more valuable your cordwood becomes. I am reminded of a story involving our gloomy and irascible mechanic, Fizzy. He had been living a perfectly misanthropic life, free of meddling, for some time when his daughter and her new husband moved in across the road. Never partial to this son-in-law, Fizzy was nonplussed at the prospect of having to share his corner of the world with the upstart.

That winter Fizzy noticed that the woodpiles lining his porch were receding faster than he knew they ought to (a stubborn, solitary Yankee with the heat needs of a Cro-Magnon knows these things almost to the stick). In his uniquely proactive fashion, he decided to use a subtle ploy to find out who was pinching his firewood. He drilled a deep hole down the center of a stick of stove wood and filled it with gunpowder (what, you don't have some under *your* sink?). He then filled the opening of the bomb with wood putty and, after sanding it smooth, returned it to the scene of the suspected thievery. Now just because Fizzy was a forgetful man does not mean that you have guessed where this story is headed, but it does explain why he was caught by surprise when his daughter's kitchen exploded some days later. There were no injuries, unless you count my gut when I heard tell.

Subversive Wood-Burners

There is an archetypal scene we almost take for granted because it is hearth and home and heritage around the hilltowns. Imagine a mountain valley on a frosty morning, early enough so that it's light but not yet sunlit. Against the snowy slopes and into the pale air rises a plume of equally pale, but closer, wood smoke from a farmhouse chimney. Classic. What's for breakfast? I hope it's black coffee, pancakes with maple syrup, and a grapefruit.

Yet that plume is pollution — visible pollution. And the saw, our hero and our loyal helper, he's not exactly an eco-paragon. Did Frank tell you the story about running a chain saw in a cellar for the 30 most tubercular seconds of his young life?

What I'm getting at is that there are those who see the Currier and Ives smoke curling from country chimneys as a threat to the environment. The Subversive Wood-Burning Culture, that's what

they call us. Firewood is blamed for everything from global warming to the gray locks of nearby Mount Greylock. Maybe the Patriot Act will someday root out all the wild-eyed, tree-toppling revolutionaries in the boondocks. Until then, I'd like to make a few points:

Thanks to catalytic and secondary combustors, stoves today are *much* cleaner than they were a generation ago.

The cord of wood you're burning contains as much heat as 150 to 180 gallons of oil (the price, in dollars, hours, or charley horses, doesn't look so bad now, does it?). To get that cord, we felled four to six trees and ran the saw for another hour and a half to limb them and buck them up. Most likely, a pickup truck made two trips (or a bigger truck made one) to bring the wood to your dooryard. Somebody swung a maul, but sweat doesn't count. Blood does, however; wars have been fought over oil fields, but not woodlots. Think of oil-well fires, pipelines exploded by terrorists,

Deutschland über woodpiles. This cottage in Germany clearly houses a subversive wood-burner. Stacking wood under the eaves will keep it dry but also brings rodents and insects closer to the house.

Vivé la resistance! To some, the plume of wood smoke from our chimney is a sign of subversion. To us, it says, "Welcome home."

drilling-rig explosions, a supertanker steaming across the ocean with the oil, or a refinery, or the all the trucks involved in getting the heating oil from a port or pipeline to your house, or a mountain leveled by strip mining.

As we leave the Oil Age and enter whatever mysterious future is ours, it looks to me like we had all better become more regionally independent and self-sufficient. Heating your house isn't a bad place to start.

There is no free heat, but the cost to those in or near wooded areas is looking lower and lower. If it's not that dirty, what makes the wood-burning culture so subversive? Sisters and brothers, I'm afraid it's . . . pleasure (gasp). A source of lively warmth is as joyful in our houses as in our hearts. Although those who come in from the cold are depicted as holding their hands out to the stove for warmth, they always soon turn and bask their butts in the glow. It feels good. The fire draws company. The hearth, the stove, the kitchen are the pulses of a country house. The fire *is* company. On a solitary evening, who sits at a desk far from the stove? We write, work, read, reflect at the kitchen table near the fire we feed, the fire that feeds us.

Those plumes of smoke from the country chimneys? Long may they wave.

5

Feel the HEAT

DAD AND I WERE RIDING AROUND in the truck the other day when it struck us that our vision of a world heated by wood might actually come to pass if fuel prices continue the way they have been. There are many who say that worldwide oil production has plateaued while the population only increases. Combine this with a national near-hysteria about exercise, and you have set the perfect stage for people to start bringing in their own firewood.

Maul Rats

Try our vision in your mind for a minute; it can't hurt. Dusk falls on a tightly packed neighborhood, and for the first time in over half a century wood smoke drifts up to meet returning workaday men and women at the corner. People come home to piles of cordwood on their lawns and in their driveways, and families work together chopping wood in the evenings rather than watching television in small clusters. There's a little time before darkness takes the suburbs and hunger takes the workers, and the neighborhood resounds with the hump and thwack of mauls as newly hardened hands whale away on the winter's firewood. The troubles and frustrations of the day go into the wood, and thence into the stove. This is a productive way to "get heated." It doesn't take long, it feels good, and you haven't delayed that first beer more than 45 minutes.

Everyone gains a better understanding of the way life used to be, and there are only two ways to take knowledge like this as far as I'm concerned. Either you will be more thankful for today's technology, if you don't like the work, or you will have a glimpse at something simpler and more self-reliant that makes you feel more alive and luckier

Haulin' ash. Splitting and stacking your own firewood is great exercise.

Burning wood with lots of resin will leave a layer of creosote in the flue, increasing the likelihood of a chimney fire.

and more connected to air and muscle than you have ever been. Everyone saves money on gym memberships and heating costs, and everyone comes to count on the smell of the first stove in the first chill of the fall. It is a smell I will never forget, one around the corner of every autumn memory, half noticed at dusk like a tendril of smoke ducking below the ridgepole in a gust of wind.

Heating with wood also takes advantage of a renewable resource. Unlike oil or natural gas, there is more firewood to be harvested responsibly in this country right now than there has been in quite some time. Sadly, the family farm is becoming a thing of the past, and all of those once carefully tended fields are filling up with one of two things: cookie-cutter housing developments or trees. Seems to me it would be better for all of us if landowners would lock up their land in conservation agreements and responsibly harvest firewood, rather than depend on an unreliable supply of oil to heat our homes.

The Tradeoffs

It is true that wood smoke is an air pollutant. However, this effect on the environment has been reduced dramatically in today's clean-burning stoves. Most on the market burn with an efficiency far under the 7.5 grams per hour of smoke regulated by the Environmental Protection Agency (EPA). Many stoves on the market burn with smoke production as low as

1 gram per hour. This is a huge improvement over the woodstoves of the past.

In contrast to the environmental impact of huge refineries and the type of ecological disaster zone we create in the Alaskan wilderness when we drill, it seems minor. Promoting a bit of a balance in the nation's energy consumption can only be a good thing. Sell your SUV and buy a chain saw and a visit from a forest-management expert.

Ways to Heat with Wood

There are a few different ways to heat with wood. If you want to use firewood, but you also want to keep the house free from the bark, soil, and other mess associated with wood, you could use an outdoor furnace. If maximum efficiency is your goal, you could have a masonry heater installed. Most people, however, will end up choosing a traditional woodstove.

Outdoor Furnaces

The outdoor furnace is a good example of what Dad likes to call "high-tech low tech." It is a simple system outdoors that requires a relatively complex system indoors. The furnace itself can be more than 100 feet from your house. It looks like a giant corrugated-metal doghouse with a little chimney on top and a blower mounted on the door. There is a large metal barrel for a firebox, which can handle 2-foot logs of any species.

The barrel is surrounded by a sleeve of water. As the fire burns in the firebox it heats the water in the sleeve; a thermostat mounted in the blower on the door keeps the water

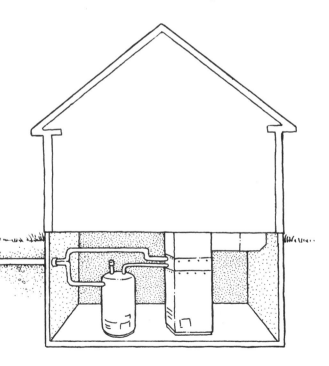

Smoking outside. The outdoor furnace burns wood to heat water for household heating. The hot water produced can also be pumped right into the plumbing system.

close to 180°F. If the water temperature drops to 160°, the blower kicks on and steps up the fire. The water is pumped from the furnace through buried, insulated pipes to the house. Once there, the water runs either through tubes that form a radiant heating system or through a heat transfer device that heats air to be blown through existing ducts. The hot water coming to the house also feeds the domestic water supply, so you are doing double duty by using this device.

The advantages of this system are less time spent on processing the firewood and more types of firewood acceptable to the system. The outdoor furnace is also a good way of keeping the dirt and general mess of the stove out of the house. There is also much less risk of burning down your house if the firebox and chimney are both outside. The downside is that a power outage will bring the whole thing to a halt.

Masonry Heaters

A masonry heater is a significant investment, no doubt. If you have the money, though, these things *will* pay for themselves. I know a man who heats a four-story house that runs 40 by 60 feet and contains a shop with a high ceiling and concrete floor using fewer than four cords a year. It is a tight, well-insulated house but has no more than the central masonry heater, which runs from the ground up, and little corner fans to put out heat all winter. Masonry heaters are just flat-out efficient. They store the heat from a small fire and throw it steadily and safely, without mechanical help, into the house all day and night. The man I spoke of tends to the fire in the masonry stove once every 24 hours.

A steady burn. A masonry heater is both beautiful and efficient, supplying slow, steady heat to any home. The wood waiter to the left is an easy way to bring wood up from the basement.

These heaters range in size from a large stove on up to massive, house-high affairs with multiple fireboxes. The outside of the heater never becomes anywhere near as hot as a traditional woodstove; rather, the heat is much more constant and comes from a much larger surface area.

Fireplaces

As we all know, fireplaces are pretty, but some people may not yet know that they are incredibly inefficient, as well as more dangerous than any of the other heating options suggested here. They are smoky, no matter what kind of wood is being burned, and there is always the risk of embers spitting from the fire into the room. Not only does the fireplace send most of its heat up the chimney, but if your house is at all drafty the fire will actually pull warm air from the room and send it up the chimney as well. On occasions when we do have a fire in our 5-foot-wide fieldstone fireplace, we can actually feel a draft curling under the doors from adjacent rooms and the sills of ill-fitting old windows.

Fires are pretty and entertaining, and fireplaces are the final repository for many a log that cannot be split by hand. They make for a good show and can be the extra entity in a room that might otherwise feel empty or awkward. I have spent as many hours in rapt attention to a fire as to any evening of television. Don't leave the room for long, though.

All about ambience. A warm hearth can be a great gathering spot, but fireplaces aren't as efficient as woodstoves at heating the house.

Woodstoves

A woodstove is a type of space heater, a device defined by the fact that it heats a space directly, rather than by air in ducts or steam in heaters. Because of this, a woodstove must be centrally located to do a good job. Not many houses are set up with the stove in the middle of the room because it is a real hindrance to the ebb and flow of daily life to have a large, incredibly hot iron appliance in the center of a room. For this reason most stoves are against a wall, but hopefully not in a corner. Ideally

LOCAL HERO

Glade Wolf stands for what we might call a hilltowner. You might have other names for it in your part of the country. This is someone who usually works alone, outdoors. Glade is a logger, landscaper, brush-hogger, wood-chipper, cordwood dealer. A lot of the time he is a man of few words. When he gets talking, he is a man of few pauses. He presents a tough face, but when he tells you about seeing a fawn up close, his face glows and his eyes are round with wonder.

Glade and I follow different paths and support different causes. Although we haven't really gotten specific, I suspect that we probably cancel out each other's vote on Election Day. A lot of the year, we don't run into each other, although if I do see him at a wedding or a funeral or the store in town, it always does my heart good.

But one day a year we work together, getting the wood in, and it is one of my favorite days. Glade used to bring his dump truck and we'd ride around the woods, from pile to pile that the boys and I had made last winter, throwing piece after piece of stove wood into the truck (which holds a cord and a quarter). Then we'd take it up to the house, dump it, and go back to the woods for more. Each load took about half an hour. Pretty soon, there'd be a huge heap of wood outside the shed waiting to be piled at leisure.

We worked hard, talking as we bent and lifted and tossed. It was by working like this that I learned all the things we have in common below the surface and beyond the bumper stickers. The best way to say it is that Glade has never lost his awe at the beauty of the workings of the animals and the trees and the humor of the workings of the human (especially, collectively and pompously, in the body politic).

Now Glade brings a tractor with a winch to our woods. The trees we felled and limbed the previous winter are secured with a logging chain and dragged up to the house where Glade neatly piles them with the tractor's bucket. From there we buck and split and stack. It is more efficient and the wood dries better in the sun, but I miss those old conversations we used to have.

the wall abutting the stove is an interior one, so that the direct heat of the stove is not going through a wall and wasting away in the outdoor wind. Most efficient setups have both a stone or ceramic hearth and a stone or ceramic wall behind the stove. This cuts down on fire hazards and absorbs and rethrows heat from the stove that would otherwise be wasted in the floor and wall.

There are two basic types of woodstoves: catalytic and noncatalytic. A catalytic stove is simply one with a device that recombusts smoke with particulate matter before it exits to the stovepipe. This device is a coated ceramic honeycomb designed to catch particles exiting the firebox that have not been thoroughly ignited. The advantage of a catalytic element

is a cleaner-burning stove that throws a more constant heat. The disadvantage is that the stove must be tended to more carefully, as it is possible to "overfire" this element and damage it. Even with careful use and regular cleaning, the catalytic element cannot be expected to remain efficient for more than six burning seasons. If the element is damaged or neglected it may not remain functional for even two seasons.

Because of the way air is introduced to the wood in a noncatalytic stove, you can achieve a faster, hotter, and, if there is a window in the stove, prettier fire. Air is preheated as it travels through vents in the bottom of the stove and is introduced at the top of the firebox. There is also a large baffle, running almost

One warm hearth. We have a medium-size soapstone stove fitted into a huge old fireplace.

all the way across the top of the firebox, that forces hot air and gases to stay in the stove as long as possible, thereby transferring heat to the stove rather than the chimney and the outside air. Noncatalytic stoves are less expensive than catalytic models, but they provide less even heat. There is more maintenance involved in running a catalytic stove than I would ever want, and I've never had any complaints about the non-cats I've used my whole life.

Running a Woodstove

A woodstove, like any other appliance in your home, must be cared for. Unlike most other appliances, the woodstove can injure you and burn down your house. You have to develop a set of habits around the stove, and then it will be not only safe and effective, but more comforting and conducive to sitting around talking than any other appliance you can think of. Who gathers with their family after dinner, leans back

A clean sweep. If you use your woodstove regularly throughout the winter, be sure to have it cleaned by a professional chimney sweep at least once a year.

in an old chair, and talks by the dishwasher? The television is in many ways the opposite of the stove, as conversation ceases in the presence of the blue-portal glow of other people's lives. There is one similarity, however: In the fall, when the stove is cold in the kitchen and the Red Sox are in the playoffs on the tube, I'm tempted to throw a heavy piece of maple into each of them.

To avoid chimney fires you should have the chimney, flue, and stovepipe cleaned by a professional chimney sweep before the first fire of the season. Here is a cautionary note to any German immigrants who may be reading this: Do not try to touch the chimney sweep for good luck without asking. I once had a German professor who dashed up to her chimney sweep and grabbed hold of him when he came to the door. Apparently in the old country it is the acme of luck to latch onto one of these fellas, reason being that anyone who spends time roof walking and ladder climbing without falling to a gruesome death is thought to be charmed. Those Germans.

Chimney fires are no joke. I was rudely awakened one winter night at the tender age of 7 and told by my breathless mother to get moving, immediately. The only logical conclusion that came to my

Choose Your Stove

Cast iron. This is a traditional material for woodstoves. It's so durable that you can find 100-year-old cast-iron stoves still being sold and used.

Enamel. For the fashion conscious, enamel-coated woodstoves come in a variety of colors.

Soapstone. Stoves made of soapstone are durable and retain heat well. This Scandinavian model has a more contemporary look than our more traditional version (see page 97).

Steel. Generally less expensive than other options, steel stoves are fine for occasional wood-burners, but they won't hold up over the long haul.

Be Generous with Elm

Stephen

Carlton and I had cut a couple of cords — pretty good stuff mostly, white birch and maple. We had bucked it up and split it and left it in the woods near the side of the road. Leaving wood can be risky. I never fully recovered from the theft, years before, of half a year's part-time work: 12 cords that I intended to sell, but left in

the woods until I could rent a truck big enough to haul a load worth the trip. When I returned to the remote landing where I had piled the wood, it was gone. The feeling of loss and remorse and foolishness was overwhelming, though not unfamiliar.

But this time, the wood was just across the road from one of Carlton's barns and a house with a tenant in it. So it seemed safe enough. We both had livestock to tend, so we agreed to meet the next weekend when our kids could help us load, unload, and stack at his house and ours. Well, on Tuesday morning Carlton peered down from the barn at our stash. And thought it looked a little shy. On Wednesday morning he looked again, and he was sure of it. So on Thursday he lay in wait. Sure enough, two cars pulled up. It was another neighbor and his grown daughter. They began to fill the trunks of their cars with the firewood.

Carlton hopped out and accosted them. "Stump, what the hell are you doing with my wood?" Stump (so nicknamed because of his graceful, willowy ways) answered, "Geez, Carl, I didn't know it was *your* land."

"My barn might have given you a clue," said Carlton, "and we've both lived here all our lives." Stump suggested, "I thought the electric company had been trimming branches along the road."

"Then how did it end up bucked and split?" asked Carlton.

Stump thought a moment, shrugged, spread his upturned palms: "Grace?" he offered.

This same woodlot was where Carlton and I also cut some elm one year. Anybody would tell you not to, but it was early November, we were both a little short of wood, and the elm was standing dead. We were too after a few days' work.

The stuff looked almost all right in rounds, but when you went to split it, the problems appeared. Mauls bounced, axes broke, and wedges were devoured whole. Basically, wood needs to have a grain before it will split. Elm has a network, a dense web of interconnected and overlapping fibers, which is probably a wonderful support system and provides important business contacts, but it admits no edge or wedge. We beat ourselves exhausted and harvested only a few pieces that looked as though they had been torn apart by an absent-minded giant. What little we took home to burn was hard to start and stingy with warmth. We left the rest for the coyotes, the porcupines, and the buzzards. I asked Carlton later: He said he'd turn a blind eye if Stump wanted to come back and steal the elm. I said I'd help the old hoser load it.

little mind was that there was a Bugs Bunny special on television. You remember the age. Imagine my surprise at finding myself knee-deep in the blowing snow of our front yard. At least I had the jarring sight of a roaring tongue of flame belching from our very own chimney to entertain me until the firefighters arrived. No lasting damage was done, unless you consider the distrust I would forever harbor for anyone yanking me out of my bed at night.

Safety

I grew up with a large Defiant in the kitchen, pumping like the heart of the house. I was small enough for years that I could lie underneath the stove while it was running very hot and draw with my crayons. This was fine, but one day I discovered how pretty the crayons were on top of the stove. They melted fast into swirled and fragrant puddles. The stains they left got right into the pores of the metal and never came out. (Water and oil can both permanently mark the top of a stove, though I don't believe this affects the amount of heat it throws.) It was a distinct pleasure of mine growing up to flick the little wads of snow that accumulate on cuffs and in hair onto the surface of a stove that is cranking along. They spit, pop, and disappear impossibly fast.

I was so comfortable around the stove that as a little boy I planted my hand firmly on its side for balance, in the summer. I must have remembered this as I stumbled once that winter and stuck out a hand for support. I got burned very badly across my palm and along all five fingers. I haven't burned my hand on a woodstove since that day over 2 decades ago.

Somehow I went along living side by side with a woodstove for almost 20 years before noticing that there is an indication of a stove's heat perceptible to the eyes as well as to the skin. I wandered into the kitchen one night after the rest of the household was peacefully prone and breathing heavily. All the lights were out, and no moon was propped in the sky to catch and agitate a powdery snow stretching away from the skirts of the house. I had just come in from the great toilet outdoors, and as such my eyes were adjusted to the dimness of the interior. The damned woodstove was glowing. I had never imagined this to be possible, but there it was, a thin pink penumbra all around the outline of the circular lid on the top of the

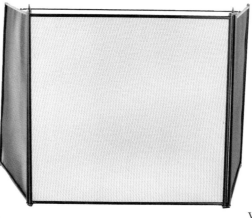

Screened in. A wire screen like this one will keep sparks in the fireplace and toddlers away from the woodstove.

stove. There was also a hazy oval on the side of the stove, threatening in its immediacy but reassuring to a mind that was soon to be 40 feet distant in a cold bed. As I watched during the next few minutes the stove became even hotter, and small imperfections in the cast iron, or bits of household detritus, began to spark and twinkle in the surface of the metal, burning off in minimal bursts of final existence.

If the notion of letting your kids burn themselves once to learn not to touch the stove seems a little harsh, you should of course get yourself a sturdy screen to keep the little firecrackers away from the heat. I have seen a number of those accordion-type expanding wooden screens for keeping both children and pets from burning themselves up. These also make top-notch clothes dryers, so have at it; the whole family may thank you.

The Laid-Back Lumberjack

Many people don't have the time, energy, or land to harvest their own cordwood the way Dad and I do. This is not to say that you couldn't just have some delivered. (It probably means you're not a true lumberjack, but who among us really is?)

Start by calling around to see who has wood for sale. Often this is a service provided by landscapers in the winter season. I will not quote any prices because they vary a good bit

1 A cord of firewood, when delivered off the back of a truck, can be tough to measure. Stack the wood and measure it to make sure you've gotten what you paid for.

2 Cribbing — lengths of wood stacked in a crosshatch — at each end of the pile will keep the wood from toppling over.

from region to region, so you can really only rely on comparisons. Have the wood delivered to your home with plenty of time to stack it or get it under cover before any snow flies. A month of solid weekends should be enough for any procrastinator.

It is often cheaper to buy wood early in the fall, before the big crush as the temperature drops. It will most likely be delivered in a dump truck of sorts, and it will come about a cord at a time, sometimes a cord and a half. Keep in mind that your lawn will take a beating if the wood is dumped there, as you won't be able to stack it all right away, and there will be a lot of bark remaining when the wood has all been stored.

What's a Cord?

There is a lot of confusing terminology floating around out there, and if you are not familiar with it, you may end up with too much, or not enough, wood when ordering from a cordwood service. Remember that a cord is 128 cubic feet of wood, when stacked. This is 4 by 4 by 8 feet, keeping in mind that only 70 to 100 cubic feet of this will be solid wood. The ratio of solid wood to volume of pile is higher when dealing with rounds rather than split wood. There is also a measurement known as a "face cord," which is simply a neat pile 4 feet tall, 8 feet long, and only 1 stick deep. This pile may also be called a "run"; it would take two runs of 2-foot pieces, three runs of

3 With completed cribbing at one end, and the first course of cribbing at the other, wood can be stacked regularly in the middle of the pile.

4 A cord, neatly stacked, should measure 4 feet by 4 feet by 8 feet.

Tips for First-Timers

If you possibly can, get your wood a year in advance, because green wood is far cheaper than seasoned, or aged, wood. If you have the room on your property to store two years' worth at all times, you'll save money by buying green cordwood and turning it into aged for free.

How do you know if wood is seasoned or green, especially if you're a little green yourself? The first clue is weight. Heft a piece of green wood and a piece of aged wood. The green is twice as heavy. Next, look at the cut ends: Fine cracks radiating out from the center of a round piece are a good sign. These cracks, called "checks" or "checking," develop as wood dries; you'll use them as guides in splitting the wood. What else? Look for peeling bark. The bark, which protects wood and keeps it green and wet, loosens in the first year, to further speed drying. Use your eyes and your nose: As wood dries, both its color and its aroma fade. Last, put your ears to work: Hit two pieces of well-seasoned firewood together, then try two green pieces. The green ones thunk, and the dry ones ring.

Some of you may be proponents of kiln-dried wood. Well-seasoned firewood from your own shed contains about 20 percent moisture, or slightly less. Kiln-dried wood is closer to 12 or 14 percent. It does light somewhat more quickly, but sometimes it also flares out too soon. The relatively minor difference in lighting slightly wetter firewood is offset by the fact that it will throw heat all night and last until morning in the stove. Kiln-dried firewood is often guaranteed bug free, if that swings your vote, but the prices I've seen at a glance were roughly twice that of regular firewood.

16-inch sticks, or four runs of 1-foot lengths to make a true cord.

How much wood you get depends on the fellas who stacked it. Recall the words of Huck Finn as he drifted past a landing on the Big Muddy: ". . . being a woodyard, likely, and piled by them cheats so you can throw a dog through it anywheres." If you're buying wood from people who stack this loosely (or throw dogs through *anything*), you might want to take your business elsewhere.

If a pile is dropped in your yard by a truck it should form a cone about 8 feet in diameter and 8 feet tall to equal a cord. These dimensions are a rough but decent gauge. You will know better how much wood you have when it is stacked, but if there's only one pile of this general size and you get billed for three cords, you know you're being hosed.

Well aged. Cordwood that's been seasoned to perfection will have telltale cracks; it will also be much lighter weight than green wood.

A Hint of Oak Aroma . . .

Frank

Along with a thousand other products one doesn't think about, firewood gets hustled into New York City in surprising amounts every day. Twenty-six to 30 tons a week of this antiquated cargo are delivered by the two men who run the Woodman — Ted and Adam. I spent a day delivering wood with them one winter.

Tucked away in corners and lofts, sometimes even behind Sheetrock, are thousands upon thousands of functioning fireplaces, many with their attendant flues reaching up and out, secret breathing tubes in airways and abandoned elevator shafts. Adam theorizes that these unexpected treasures are enabled by the predominance of masonry in Manhattan construction. According to his theory, whereas most cities have to worry about fire in many of their wooden row houses, New York does not. So in the end, it all comes back to the universal conviction that landlords act only when they have to: No chimneys were disabled because no fires were feared, and never you mind the squirrels and pigeons plumbing these former hotspots.

All but one of our score of clients that day were men, and most were loving the rugged, atmospheric upgrade their lives were receiving with the delivery of firewood. Problem is, firewood comes from a big old plant, grown in dirt and covered in unruly bark. It can have bugs and clumps of dirt picked up while being skidded out of the woods. Though the kiln-dried cordwood the Woodman sells is bug free, we did have a complaint about the "overbearing odor" of some

of the wood. Adam's response: "The product can have a scent. I suspect what you're noticing is the hickory, which some barbecue places actually pay extra for."

Mostly customers just flat baffled me by talking about stove wood like red wine all day. It was variously praised as having delicate aromas, good acrid smells, and mixtures of flavor. Thoreau is on a rotisserie in his grave, I thought, and I had to keep clearing laughter from my throat while lurching for the freight elevators with a load of wood.

We finished with the Upper East Side and headed south, away from the vaulted ceilings and stooped maids. A few deliveries to slightly more cramped families in the Village (the wood had to go right next to the hot tub on the roof patio) and it was beer-o-clock. We slumped against the scraped and naked sideboards in the back of the truck, legs out straight, feet crossed in defiance of another burdened step. Red Stripe followed anecdote upon pizza and then Red Stripe, and we were laughing in the sulfur light and little drifts of bark. I hope that at least a few of the Woodman's clients were just then enjoying the miniature skyline of their feet, one over the other, silhouetted by new fire.

6 Burn, Baby, BURN

MOST PEOPLE HAVE SPENT at least a little time in their lives near an open flame. In my experience it doesn't take long before even those indisposed to daydreaming begin to wonder at humans' domestication of fire.

Likely you will agree that there is something hypnotic and comforting about a fire. For me there is also something akin to a mothering instinct. I feel a very visceral desire to feed and build and protect a small fire. Every once in a while, I want to let a little fire eat as much as it pleases and grow to 20 feet high.

Starting a Fire

Most likely, though, your first foray into fire starting will be in a woodstove. In order to get a fire burning hot, there are a few steps you need to follow.

You should have some kindling (small, thin, dry pieces of wood that catch fire quickly) and some larger pieces of dry wood on hand. Now, if you are a good, hard worker like me it will take you only another 20 minutes to make a fire. This is because you'll have some things called paper knots (locally referred to as "Nantucket knots"; see page 111) to get the fire started.

When all of your tinder is ready, get active with the flint. You would be hard pressed to find anyone who still uses a flint and tinder in the original sense. A piece of flint was struck against a little bit of rough metal, and the resulting spark fell into a little pile of fluffy burning material like birch bark torn into strips (the tinder). The fire was then coddled and fed from this little spark. We still use flint and tinder, but again, in a small, contained form. There is actually a tiny cylinder of flint held with a spring against the underside of a rough metal wheel, all inside the little metal housing atop your standard lighter. Go ahead and use this ingenious little device; no one will judge you harshly, though it is quite satisfying to run a strike-anywhere match along the top of the stove and toss it into the open stove even as it flares to life.

Stuff a few of the light paper knots into the stove, making sure to leave them arranged loosely enough that lots of air can get at them. Next, put on a few of the heavier knots and top them off with some thin kindling. The kindling should be something light and easily split into thin strips, like white pine or ash. Light the thin paper knots in as many places as you can reach, and then set the stove at its airiest setting. If it is a top-loading affair, open both vents and leave the lid a little askew. If it is a side- or front-loading stove, open the vent on the back all the way and leave the door ajar, but only if you aren't going to leave the room. Once the paper has burned out from underneath the kindling there should be enough room, and flame, to put in some larger pieces of cordwood. (See illustrations below for an alternate technique.)

There it is, fire in a box. When it gets roaring right along, shut down the flaps and vents, as you have been promoting a hot fire. However, the massive airflow has been pulling

1 To build a fire in a woodstove, begin by laying three smallish pieces of wood (about the size of your forearm, unless you're Popeye) as shown above, with a pile of newspaper knots under a tepee of kindling in the center.

2 After you light the fire, place another smallish piece of wood on the two bottom pieces, forming a log cabin.

A good fire and a friendly dog. The only thing missing is a mug of hot cocoa.

much of the fire's heat up the chimney. When you shut the stove down, the fire inside will really start to heat the metal, or ceramic, on the outside of the stove, and thus your house. One last warning: If you have a silly dog with long hair, she will try to lick your hands and walk in little circles and not notice that all of her fur is burning slowly and making your kitchen smell like a tire yard.

3 As the fire builds, continue to add larger pieces of wood in the log-cabin style. This will give the fire some stability and keep the burning wood from collapsing in on itself.

Burning through the Night

The trickiest part of heating your home with a woodstove is the long stretch of time when you are sleeping, and in most cases, the even longer stretch of time when you are off at work. To combat this you must become a master of "banking" your stove. This means piling it full of the longest-burning pieces you can find (dense, large, hardwood bolts) and shutting all of the vents as much as possible without choking off the fire. When getting to know a new stove you will invariably wake up some mornings to a cold, empty firebox after allowing the stove too much air overnight, and some mornings to a firebox jammed full of cold, unburned, smoked firewood. This last is a result of too little air in the firebox. When you get it just right, you will have a good bed of coals to stir up in the morning, and sometimes you can go for as long as a week without having to start a fire from scratch.

As you approach master status, the life cycle of the firebox begins to reveal itself to you, and you notice that by letting the fire burn down a little in the hours leading up to your bedtime you can fit much more wood in the stove when it comes time for the final banking. If it burns down too much, however, there will not be sufficient coals to get all of the new wood going in the somewhat oxygen-deprived atmosphere of the nighttime stove. Many people with a woodstove treat it a bit like a baby and get up to perform fumbled tendings in the night.

A wood furnace is much like a stove, only the phases of the cycle are slower and longer. Furnaces can hold much more and much larger wood, and most have more sophisticated airflow systems. Because of that, they can go a lot longer without human attention.

Making Nantucket Knots

This type of knot is made of old newspapers, and it has become clear to me that newspapers are like fine wine. When they first arrive at your house there is nothing good in there at all, and you throw them on the pile with all the other old newspapers. Then you turn your back, and the fermentation of content begins. Aided by pressure and time, the little bits of interesting information are leached out of the front pages, back pages, and even inserts. All of this trickles down the stack, taking things of even more interest as the process continues, until sometime in December you are running late in the freezing dark morning, and you stand next to an open, cold stove and come across the five most unbelievably intriguing articles of all time. "So that's what happened to John F. Kenne—," you shout just as you are distracted by a foolproof way to turn packing peanuts into platinum.

To the Ash Heap

If you're starting a fire in a stove that's seen some action, you'll need to clean out most of the ash first. Scoop out enough ash so there is plenty of room in the firebox, but still an inch or so in the bottom to protect the metal firebox from being dented when new pieces of wood are dropped in. If the stove was running even as recently as the previous day the coals might still be hot. Every year a few houses in the Hilltowns are burned up completely by people shoveling out their stoves and putting the ashes somewhere unsafe. Throw them in your driveway or on your front walk for traction, put them in a metal container away from all walls and newspaper or other possible fuel, or douse them in water. Anything is better than letting these tricky little gray opossums flare back to life and light something.

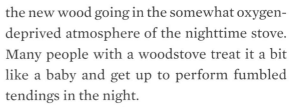

I have given up and now make all my paper knots in the dark. Every winter all over New England Red Sox fans talk about the next baseball season. This collective chatter is called the Hot Stove League. I submit to you now that everyone making their own fires is standing in front of an unlit stove every morning, looking at old sports pages, and unwittingly participating in the much larger, more solitary Cold Stove League. Once you've caught up on all the amazing things newly printed in the old paper (I know those articles were not there the first time), you can commence making your knots.

Shake loose a full two-page section, that is, the large sheet that when folded makes four pages of text. Turn the whole thing horizontally so that both of your hands are along the top of the page (gleefully gripping a headline about the Yankees losing) and roll it up tightly. You should have a tube with the two edges of the paper running its length. Now simply tie this into a big pretzel-like knot. This will be a very fast-burning knot, so make a few of these and then start making your knots with more pages, even a whole section if it's thin enough to tie after being rolled. These knots should go into the fire second and will burn for a surprisingly long time if rolled and tied tightly. Standing in the dark, rolling newspaper furiously one day and contemplatively the next has become part of my memory of childhood.

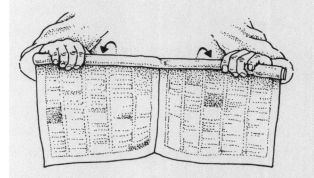

1 Open a full section of the least interesting part of the newspaper. (The business section is perfect. Do not use the comics, the sports section, or Dear Abby, or you'll hamper your progress considerably.) Roll it lengthwise, as shown.

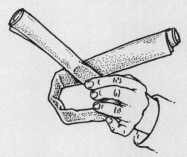

2 When the newspaper achieves a tubelike state, fold it into a small loop.

3 Tie the loop into your standard knot (no Boy Scout training needed), and toss it in the woodstove. If you're thinking ahead, you'll make a whole pile of knots at a go for the next time you have to start a fire.

Fire Pits

No backyard is complete without a little fire pit. If you are going to burn leaves or dead branches for cleanup purposes, or even have the occasional bonfire, you should have a little pit for the occasion. Take safety into account above all else, and pick a spot farthest removed from your house and any other structure. Barring a strong, consistent wind bearing fire back toward the house, this is your best spot for a fire pit. Keep in mind also that even relatively small fires (say, 3 to 6 feet tall) will burn all of the foliage from any branches hanging in a 50-foot vertical column above the fire pit. I know this from a pretty spicy experience with a tall, leaning locust in our backyard. Often just the heat from the fire is enough to damage a tree's limbs, even if they don't catch fire.

You must also consider whether there are roots running under your site. This may sound farfetched, but I personally know a woman who almost burned down a whole grove of pines with a few candles amidst the roots of an old spruce. Fire can actually burn along the inside of dead or especially pitch-filled roots. Choose the size of your fire pit based on a rather complicated trigonometric theory: Make its diameter the same as the height of the fires you will be having. Dig out a circle 6 to 8 inches deep, and flip all the sod. The sod can stay in the circle; you just want to chop out and remove any tree roots that might transport flames to nearby woods. Line the perimeter of your pit with the stones you will inevitably find. If you don't find any stones in the ground, write your name and address on a 3-by-5 card and send it to me. Better yet, box up all of the dirt on your property and just send it to my garden.

One last safety note: I know a lot about wood and only a little about stones, but I do know that many rocks have little bits and pockets of water trapped in them. In a hot bonfire, I have seen these rocks explode with amazing force, throwing shards of stone and ashes into the air. I don't know how to avoid this, other than having a few small fires first. This will give the stones a chance to heat up slowly rather than going straight to a thousand degrees in 20 minutes for the first time in 500,000 years. You'd pop, too.

S'mores, anyone? Our bonfires get bigger than this (turn the page), but the average homeowner should stick to smaller fires.

The Backyard Bonfire

The tepee method is an easy way to lay wood for a bonfire, especially if you have long pieces.

The log cabin method sometimes calls for a larger fire pit (or smaller pieces of wood), but it tends to be more stable than the tepee method.

Bonfires should always be sited in an area that's been cleared of fallen debris, away from nearby trees and shrubs. Always be sure to have buckets of water on hand to douse any sparks that fly outside the fire pit.

Digging a pit surrounded by a shallow trench will help keep the fire contained.

Bonfire of the Vanities (and Dressers and Staircases . . .)

We have an annual New Year's Eve bonfire, and over the years it has become a community event. All year people bring old dressers, brush, and couches up to a well-scarred spot in our field and drop them all off. There is one man in particular who really gets into the spirit of giving, and he has been known to come down the driveway dragging some ratty branch or piece of furniture, with a cigar in his mouth and a grin on his face. During the New Year's Eve blowout of 2001, his barrel-chested form came softly out of the gloaming and, with a shout of good cheer, knocked a handful of my college buddies flat on their butts in the middle of our decorative little pond. Neighbors like these are worth their weight in roast pig.

Some people will tell you that gasoline is the way to get a fire really ripping. When employing any volatile substance, especially gasoline (which has an incredibly low and fast flash point), remember this above all else: Do not add more of the volatile substance while the fire is burning. Even if you think the fire has gone out and wish to juice it back up again, you have lost the right to use more gas. Even a

1 The beginnings of our bonfire include random brush, construction debris from a friend's house, and a few logs.

2 Just one more log, and maybe a few Christmas trees for good measure . . .

tiny ember or unseen flame will be enough to ignite the new gasoline. Once lit, you cannot imagine how fast flames move through gasoline if you've not seen it. Gas can burn right back up the stream as fast as you can throw it. If there is any gas on your shoes, pants, or hands, the fire will jump there instantly. I have seen too many people come close to bad burns or explosions to let this point go lightly. Given all of the risk, it really is not worth it or necessary to use gas to start a bonfire.

Arrange the spot you wish to burn best in the bonfire, a place you've kept dry or stocked with dry wood. Make sure there's ample fuel already in place above and on the side of the pile the wind is blowing toward. Make a nest of crumpled newspaper or birch bark. The latter is actually quite a bit more flammable and enduring. Make sure that there is a progression of larger fuel above this nest and closer to the center of the pile. Flame wants to travel upward, and any wind you may encounter will just drive the flames deeper into the heart of the pile. Use these two things to your advantage, as you will have to start over if your flames burn out all the nearby fuel and do not advance to the heart of the pile. Absolutely avoid having a starting point that requires any

3 I briefly consider adding this giant spool to the pile but save it for birling practice instead.

4 Connie uses her homemade blowtorch (see page 116) to get the fire started.

serious reaching. I've been tempted to cut a tunnel to the heart of a pile and get in there to feed the fire. This is a bad idea. You should be able to light the fire and take a long stride away immediately. Only go back in close if the flames are starving for fuel (which shouldn't be necessary if you've played the wind and the trail of fuel correctly).

For those with deep pockets and an all-natural inclination, there is a substance known as "fatwood." True fatwood is split from the remains of ancient, southern long-leaf pine trees and is taken from stumps and logs of the very same that may have been curing for over a hundred years. Just a few thin pieces of this wood contain a volatile resin that will burn with the intensity and duration necessary to start any fire. I've used the stuff and know that it works quite well, but I do feel silly paying top dollar to have some guy in seventy-five-degree heat ship my snowbound butt some firewood.

I often insist that my stepmother intervene in the lighting of a good-size fire. She is a peaceable, reasonable woman who makes her living molding clay from the earth. She is also an inveterate pyromaniac and once hauled a propane tank hooked to a homemade flame-thrower round and round the base of a 10-foot mountain of dry pine and wainscoting. Forty minutes later we were scratching together another pile of wood so as not to disappoint that evening's guests.

Safe Burning

Much like an automobile, a fire can be far easier to get going than to stop. Our biggest fires take place in a few feet of snow, so things really can't get too far out of hand. However, everyone out there isn't blessed (cursed?) with a deep New England winter. When we have put on big fires in any of the summer months we

One hot mama. Connie normally uses her propane-fired blowtorch in her pottery studio, but she also puts it to use on bonfire night every year.

have taken a number of precautions. We keep between six and a dozen 5-gallon buckets full of water in a loose ring around the fire. We have the fire within 100 feet of a pond in our back field, and one particularly dry year I got a truckload of sand from the highway department and heaped a rough ring around the fire pile, at a distance of about 10 feet. One more piece of advice: If you live anywhere near other folks, call your fire chief and obtain his permission for a fire. Many sparsely populated places have fire towers, and if alerted these fellows will rest easier knowing that smoke on the horizon comes from an intentional and controlled fire.

When it comes to putting out the remains of a fire before bedtime, planning is everything. You should have stopped adding wood long ago, so as to be contending only with a pile of coals. There have been years when we have had to douse a 3-foot pile of white-glowing embers before bed. Provided it is still dark, the lack of light is your ally. Grab one of those buckets and start sloshing. When all the red is gone, go kick around in the pile; you will be amazed at how much heat and potential fire remain. Repeat the task until you can't stir up even the dimmest of sparks. This last hunt is best conducted with the old human fire engine, and you should have been stocking up your tank with beer for this very occasion.

Hotter than blazes. Who brought the hot dogs?

Don't Try This at Home

As New Year's Eve approached one year, the family began to spin out into its usual loops of crazed and primitive behavior. My step-mother would walk through a room muttering about whether old kerosene became denatured, and Dad decided it was time I learned truly precise and responsible tree felling. He took me up to the hillside where we were to have the pig roast that year and pointed to a little copse near the top. It contained some young hardwoods and the inevitable bare rock that allows this type of growth in a mowed field. Among the trees was a single, towering white pine. It stood 70 feet and, by virtue of being uphill, was 10 to 12 feet above the top of the bonfire pile.

"I'd love to burn that thing," said the Rip-Roarin' Rev, knowing he didn't mean what I thought he meant.

"Sure, let's drop it, buck it into four-foot lengths, and toss it in," I said innocently. Not used to being the responsible one, I was stubbornly resisting the idea I now feared imminent.

"No, no, what if we drop it right onto the fire while it's ripping along?"

I had to admit that this appealed to everything stupid in my soul (which doesn't leave a whole helluva lot left over). We lined it up as best we could, never having had to drop a tree so precisely down such a hill. He thought it sighted just fine, but the grouping of branches along the northeast side of the trunk had me chewing the inside of my cheek before sleep came that night.

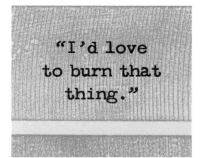

"I'd love to burn that thing."

The next day, I went out and moved the entire pile, piece by piece, a couple of yards in the direction the preponderance of branches were growing. By flashlight, up to our thighs in light, powerfully cold snow, and at the stroke of midnight, the Rev dropped that tree directly on the roaring spine of a great fire. The resulting air rush asphyxiated the thing for one silent moment, only to have the fire roar to life, and the crowd along with it. Mark one for the Rev.

One year our friend Nate pulled off one of the greatest New Year's bonfire stunts I know of. Being the waste-not-want-not arsonist that I am, I put an entire 20-step wooden staircase from an old mill in my truck and took it home. It didn't sit in the snow by the fire for more than 15 seconds before I had switched its role in my head from "thoughtful seating for contemplative guests" to "possible staircase into the depths of hell."

I waited until Nate was "sensible," which is easier to say than "insensate" anyway, and then asked him if he would be willing to hoist a bone-dry, 11-foot-tall Christmas tree over his head, run up the staircase propped on the fire itself, and plant the tree directly in the highest crags of the inferno at the stroke of midnight. This is what passes for a "moment" around our neck of the woodlot. He muttered a quick and eager "yes" through his tears of gratitude.

At 11:57 p.m. Dad and I humped the staircase over and rammed it against one side of the fire. Moments later, the traditional "NASA blastoff" chant began. With Dad holding his belt from behind (as a safety measure), Nate staggered up to the top of the new flight, said something about it being "hot" up there, and dumped the tree onto the blazing fire, to rousing cheers from below.

A Lumberjack's Pig Roast

Frank

I do not cook. In some circles, I am not even *permitted* to cook. However, once a year I make a bigger, cheaper, better-tasting meal than some chefs ever will. I know that this sounds unlikely, but only because you don't know that this meal comes by the graces of an animal by the name of "pig." Each year for the past 7 years I have roasted a pig with the help of family and friends on New Year's Eve. The pig is the perfect animal for a roast, even for rank amateurs. And believe me, even if you are a good-smelling amateur, you will be rank by the end of a pig roast.

Here is how we do it: Count in your head, or on your abacus if you're too addled, the number of people coming to your roast. Turn the word "people" into the word "pounds." This is how big your pig needs to be *after* it has been cleaned. In other words, the weight it's going to be when it goes on the spit. This complex algorithm works for anywhere between 15 and 35 people, in my experience. My only gross miscalculation came in the horrifying chasm of waste between 80 guests at a tony garden party and the 85-pound hog named Brad, whose head, complete with chef's toque, sat on a pole nearby and laughed. Or cried. It was tough to tell. Either way, there was enough pig left over to shoot a banquet scene for *Beowulf*. My theory is that people were not sufficiently hungry, and that as the hog gets bigger, the ratio of pig weight to edible meat is far closer to one to one. Some of the little guys we've done had almost half their body weight locked up in inedible hocks and bonds, like bones and head (though the cheeks can be quite good).

You will need an absolute, outside maximum of one-half cord of good hardwood to cook your pig. This may seem like a lot, and it really is, but we've learned the hard way that it's good to have extra wood on hand. One year the air temperature on New Year's Day was below zero, and a wind was blowing. The temperature kept the top side of the pig cool, and the constantly shifting wind actually kept the flames out from underneath the little trotter. We dropped the spit down real low and stoked the blaze like firemen in an old-fashioned locomotive race, and the pig was delicious, but it ate $50 worth of wood before we got a chance to return the favor.

One way to avoid this problem, somewhat, is to have a supply of cinder blocks lying around, and to bank them up on the windy side of the fire or coals. They will serve the dual purpose of blocking wind and absorbing and then reflecting heat back to the pig. Do not try to build anything with these blocks later, though, as extreme heat has caused all of my blocks to become very brittle. While on the subject of equipment, let me stress that you need not spend much time or money at all on the essentials. I took an 8-foot length of 1½-inch iron pipe and crimped one end by cutting out darts with a hacksaw and pounding the remaining flanges into a point. I found a rugged-looking gear from some old machinery that must be about 14 inches across and pounded it onto the untouched end of the iron pipe. Then I drilled a number of holes through both walls of the pipe out near the middle, and these I used to pound stainless-steel rods through the hips and shoulders of the pig and spit, to keep the spit from just spinning as the heavy side of the pig stays downward. The spit simply sits on two metal fence posts with stout loops of wire hanging down from their tops. Burnish the spit every few years, and leave the grease on the spit after a roast. It keeps any rust from forming, and you simply wash the bejesus out of the thing on the day of the roast the next year.

The trick to a good even roasting, without a lot of smoke hitting the pig and without the pig catching fire too much, is to roast over coals and not naked flame. (Relax if the pig does catch fire, and do not throw water on the poor thing, because doing so will not help. If the pig catches too badly, for more than a minute, remove it from the fire and pat out the flames with a towel or long beard.) To get a deep, resilient bed of coals, you need a second fire. This is why having a bonfire ripping nearby is so useful at a pig roast. We toss the hardwood to be used in cooking in a pile at a point on the bonfire's periphery where it can easily be raked underneath the pig when the fire has reached the stage of hot charcoal. This way the heat is steady, clean, and predictable.

Give the pig a quarter turn every 20 to 30 minutes; two or three times throughout the process, offset the turn by 45 degrees, so that even heat is applied to the whole pig. When it comes down to the wire, you need to be gentle with the pig, as it will get very loose in the joints and even fall apart sometimes. This is good, and a pork-fueled conflagration can be avoided by wrapping the pig in chicken wire before cooking. This has always seemed a little much to me, and we usually just put a 2- by 4-foot stainless-steel grill on cinder blocks under the spinning pig during the last hour over the heat.

You must keep a meat thermometer around, and after 5 or 6 hours of good sizzling, start to check the temperature in the deepest meat, in the center of the front shoulder and the center of the hams. This meat will be the last to reach a safe temperature for eating; you will want the most reluctant meat to reach at least 145°F, and don't worry if those last 10 degrees or so take quite a while. It is not a steady climb you should aspire to, but rather to reach the top. Someone might actually have said that, so there's your dose of culture for the week.

Remember to keep an eye on the more delicate regions as well, such as the loin. This is the (hopefully) long stretch of meat laid along either side of the spine between the last rib and the hips. The loin gets a lot of heat because of its central location, and it has much less fat insulating it than either the shoulders or the hams. I have taken a pig from the fire before the hams were done right to the bone in order to keep the loin from overcooking, and nobody in their right mind complained. It may have been due to the cleavers and chain saws lying around, though.

CHAPTER 7

Logger Games

I HAVE A CONFESSION: Much of this book was written in a cramped apartment in Brooklyn, New York. Everyone knows that this is a tough town for actors and writers and strivers of every type, but the plight of the urban lumberjack has not yet been sung. There is nothing to chop and nothing to fell. There is nothing to split or stack.

A Lumberjack in the Concrete Forest

It wears on me to have to release physical energy in a way that does not produce anything. I run and bike and generally thrash around as much as I can within the realm of social normalcy, but it just isn't the same. So it has come to pass that I must train for lumberjack contests in a concrete forest, where it's easiest to find trunks in the zoo and limbs in the river.

I have had one hell of a time finding unspoken-for wood to chop and saw. My first attempts were undertaken in a manner against my nature, that is, through the proper channels. This method turned out to be quite entertaining, somewhat educational, and totally fruitless. So, I took it in my own hands to find some unwatched wood. I went down to the east bank of the East River. Once there, I picked my way along its tortured "shore," which is more man than nature, bristling with abandoned concrete jetties and sagging creosote piers. Most of a mile later I came sweating to a section of relatively natural pebbles and stones between a vacant lot and the water's edge. In true city fashion, everything by the water's edge was in layers and divisions, and separating the shore from the lot was a sort of giant's high-water mark

Training up. Who would have thunk, thunk, thunk it? Free wood in sight of the Empire State Building (these old pilings stank like crazy).

composed of bleached pilings and old timbers in a rough jackstraw fringe parallel to the river. This was what I had been hoping for, and before anyone could talk me out of it, I whacked my ax into the first clear-looking timber I saw, parallel with the grain. I pulled out my file and set to sharpening the edge of the bit facing skyward.

I practiced chopping for almost 2 hours that first day by the river and was too tired even to try the one-man bucksaw. It sat in the

sun on the roots of an old brick pier, if you can imagine such a thing, and absorbed so much solar heat that I had trouble finding a way to carry it the 13 blocks back to my place.

Here is as good a place as any to relate the narrow wisdom I've compiled regarding travel with obvious tools of destruction (or construction, for that matter). You might initially assume, as I did, that moving around a large city, particularly one as jumpy about terrorism as New York, with an ax and a large saw would be difficult and stress laden. Not so, for I quickly adopted the excuse that I was in a movie, and a few people even spun quickly on the off chance that I meant *right then, I was in a movie*. This excuse was fine for most, but those who knew enough to tell a well-used tool from some chintzy prop needed a bit more reassurance that I wasn't harvesting heads, so I told them the truth.

When you have lived in the city long enough, you learn to turn off large portions of your brain when you find that you are engaged with a crazy person. I had never experienced that look from the other side until the week I spent humping an ax and saw around Brooklyn, in ninety-plus heat, covered in sweat and wearing the only pants I own light enough for the weather. These pants are covered in spatters of dark red paint from work on an old barn years previously. Why I didn't stop myself at the door before leaving is a mystery, but not as deep a mystery as why I'm not writing this from behind some variety of bars. At any rate, it takes a bit of hassle, and a lot of faith on behalf of your fellow man, but you really can just stroll around New York City with an ax.

The Origins of Logging Sports

The people I've mentioned throughout the book who make their living from felling trees and hauling them to sawmills are loggers. Loggers used to be called lumberjacks, but in modern times this last term has been co-opted by a sect of athletes who compete in traditional timber sports. These are activities that used to be essential parts of a lumberjack's job, or at least playful extensions thereof (thinking now of ax throwing, the utility of which would take some really creative explaining).

The skills needed for felling trees varied from region to region because of the kinds of trees being logged. Whereas loggers on the East Coast had plenty of reasonably clear rivers through which to pump their lifeblood, loggers on the West Coast had turbulent, cataract-filled rivers and no snow cover for skidding. In addition, these men were felling trees immensely larger than anything toppling at the hands of East Coast loggers.

Thus the western loggers had a whole legion of specialized tasks and techniques unused by lumberjacks in other regions, and many of these skills are still represented in

This old-timer heads out to cut with a two-man felling saw and a double-bitted ax.

A string bean with braces stands atop his springboard plank and goes to work with an ax.

national lumberjacking competitions. In a West Coast logging camp at the dawn of the twentieth century you could expect to find fallers, buckers, snipers, swampers, hooktenders, and teamsters. Because of the massive flare at the bottom of the trunks of giant Douglas firs and redwoods, it was actually more efficient for loggers to cut through the tree at a point just above the flare, even though this could be 6 to 12 feet above the forest floor.

Loggers would put small planks end first into specially chopped notches in the trunk a few feet below the desired cutting spot. (This is the origin of the competitive discipline called the "springboard chop.") Then these fellas, known as fallers, would chop, or by the 1880s saw, through the trunk and leap or scramble clear as the giant keeled over. At this point, buckers would use two-man bucksaws to cut the tree into manageable logs. Snipers would then use axes to lop any limbs or knots from the lead end of each log and whack

a quick point on it so that it would not snag on any of the numerous hindrances jutting from the typical forest floor. Swampers were responsible for clearing and maintaining the paths used to get logs out to the "skid roads." These were roads constructed of logs laid parallel to the direction of travel, over which teams of mules, horses, or oxen dragged bundles of logs.

The teamster and the hooktender were responsible for the travels of the timber. The hooktender was in charge of the array of lines as well as block and tackle used to help the teams of animals dragging the timber through the unpaved forest. In more modern and universal terms, this guy is called the "choke setter" or "choker setter," so named because he loops the cable around the log before it is pulled from the woods. The cable is of a choker style, for it tightens as it is tugged. The teamsters (so named for the teams of animals they tended and drove) were perhaps the most universal of the workers in a logging operation, in that they were represented in myriad other industries as the people who moved the goods from the forest, field, or pier to their next destination. These terms are all argot, and probably changed from job site to job site, if the logging industry is anything like farming or card games.

Old-time team. A team of draft horses hauls a load of logs out of the forest on a sledge.

Lumberjacking Events

Many of the skills that logging jobs used to require live on in lumberjack competitions around the country, from the small local agricultural fair to the granddaddy of them all, the Stihl Timbersports Series. After sharpening my skills along the banks of the East River, I decided to compete in the lumberjack games at a few regional fairs in Maine. Detailed here are some of the events I observed and participated in that summer.

Standing Block Chop

A block roughly 10 inches in diameter has to be chopped all the way through with the fewest number of strokes. In the event of a tie (quite common), time is the determining factor. Since the competitors are all so close in ability, the blocks are frequently cut through in the same number of strokes, and the contest has really become a race, rather than a stroke-counting event. In the year 2000, a world record was set as a man cut through a round of cottonwood 1 foot in diameter in 14 seconds. These fellas can swing it. This event is just not done that often at the smaller shows, and no one could really tell me why. I got all the vertically mounted chopping I could handle in the springboard chop, though (see page 130), and with terrible footing 7 feet off the ground in the bargain. Maybe I'll come across a standing block chop event in my future lumberjacking pursuits across the country.

1 Arden Cogar Jr., a regular competitor on the national circuit, lays into a trunk during the standing block chop . . .

2 . . . and finishes it off with one last whack.

Underhand Block Chop

A standard 10-inch-diameter block is clamped horizontally this time, and the competitor must chop it in half while standing on it. A few swings are to be taken at one side, then the competitor must turn around and chop the rest of the way through from the other side. This event actually had me most concerned, as it calls for the head of the ax to be whistling at a target less than 3 inches from my feet while I'm trying to balance just above.

When I competed in this event at the Woodsman's Field Day in Clinton, Maine, a guy by the name of Rich Jordan sort of took me under his wing, I think just to be nearby when whatever ridiculous thing I was obviously going to do actually went down. I was nailing my block to some 2-by stock, using my ax as a hammer and generally being happy and clueless. He came over with a hammer, looked down, and said, "Why don't you go bury that thing in the woods?" I looked around to see whether he meant my friend John Henry but quickly realized that he meant my ax. He asked how it felt to get hit in the gut all the time by the end of a handle that was obviously 6 inches too long.

1 I wait on the block, eyeing my first shot, while the timer gets set.

2 It's crucial to turn your body from the feet up, so that each swing is the same, whichever side of the cut you're working one.

I admitted that my form was not as graceful as it could be, and he showed me why — it was obvious by his first few pantomimed swings that I had been standing far too upright upon contact and getting my wrists all tangled by the long handle. His practice ax was to hand, and he told me to find a worse block, if possible, and give it a try with the shorter handle and heavier head, not to mention a blade that made mine look like a snow shovel.

He told me to give it a rip but stopped me the instant my ax hit the wood. I could see immediately that I had hit the block between

3 One more stroke on this side, and then it's a quick jump-turn to come through with a few shots to the "far wood."

my feet almost perpendicular to the grain, right on but way out of line with the angle he had traced. He said, "You've been splitting too much wood." These are words one can be proud of hearing in only one place in the world, and I was in that place. If this guy thought I had been splitting too much wood, then brother, it was too much wood.

I had started the ax off my right-hand hip and come down from over my right shoulder. He said that if I took only one thing from this lesson it was to always swing in a line down the center of my body, starting up above my head and finishing with my hands way down between my knees. If I needed to chop at an angle to the wood, then I had only to turn on my heels until my feet were parallel to the desired cut. This made good sense, and I started again. This time I remembered what Rich had told me, followed his sequence, and chewed my way through the front side.

Gentle reader, unless you've done it right, you don't know the absolute visceral satisfaction of popping a piece of wood twice in sharp succession and then watching as a chip the size of your forearm flies free to reveal the next obstacle between you and the clock. I turned more nimbly than I had expected to the other side and came through with four or five fewer hits, guessing correctly which one would sever the block and skipping free of the flipping halves. This was my first real underhand chop, and I was hooked.

Springboard Chop

A competitor chops a quick notch into a 9-foot-tall pole about 3 feet up and places a plank with a tapered metal cap (called a "shoe") into the notch. These shoes have a slight upward lip at their terminus that grabs the ceiling of notch to make the plank stable enough to stand on. The competitor then climbs up onto the plank, repeats the process 6 feet up, and then must repeat the process of the standing block chop atop his last plank. This time, the block must be struck from both sides before it falls, requiring the ax wielder to swing both left- and right-handed.

1 Jumping from plank one to plank two takes confidence in your notches. The ax waits patiently in the doomed block.

2 My plank was not seated perfectly and began to sag. As a result, each hit was harder, and higher up, than the last.

Ideally, the notch that holds the springboard is cut in four strokes. When done properly the notches hold the springboards quite safely, though there is usually some sagging as the end of the springboard bites into the ceiling of the notch. This is inevitable in soft wood, if you consider the fulcrum involved: You have a person, often well over 200 pounds, standing on a board in a notch only 3 to 4 inches deep, so even if the top of the tip is held at the very deepest part of the pocket, the lever arm is only 4 inches long on the holding side, and 4 feet long on the weight side. It's amazing the boards hold as well and as

often as they do. Chopping through a 10 by 10 on the ground is hard enough, but once your feet are 7 feet from the ground and at some sort of angle (sharp uphill tilts are as common as severely sagging springboards), the whole enterprise gets much dicier.

One year at our local fair, a 70-year-old man was left in midair when his second springboard popped out of a hastily cut notch. As he fell, he threw his razor-sharp ax away from his body. Everyone rushed to his side, but he hopped up in sudden fashion and went directly to scrutinize the blade for nicks. Needless to say, he was my hero for the week.

3 This is not a look of triumph, but rather the look of a man who might toss out a lung at any minute. Notice the top plank's final angle, compared to the optimistic horizontal I began with. Lesson learned.

In Search of Springboard Shoes

In addition to running the lumberjack contest at our local fair, Mark Gould manufactures springboard shoes: black metal caps that cover the business end of the springboard. The very tips of the shoes are hollow ground from behind, so that they curl up to a sharp little blade all the way across the 3-inch tip. When jammed into the right kind of notch, these upward-facing blades hold tight in the sloping roof of the notch and do not budge. I knew this to be true because they had been reliably supporting Mark, who to use his words "runs about two-forty to two-fifty." This is a good 50 to 60 pounds more than I go, and I had no doubts about hopping onto these planks if only I could make the right notch to hold them.

HEAVYWEIGHT

Another heavyweight in attendance at one of the competitions was a Quebecois named Gaston Duperre. I don't think this dude had a choice about what he was going to be. "Paging Dr. Duperre, Dr. Gaston Duperre to surgery." Somehow this just doesn't work, and if you ever clapped eyes on this guy, you'd agree. He is one of the strongest men I saw in my travels, built for pure power at 5'8" and just over 200 pounds. He showed himself to be quite nimble too, and I was surprised he didn't finish in the money much more than he did. He was the overall champion woodsman in 2004 at Fryeburg and the Stihl Timbersports Series overall champion in 1989. He's been competing for 26 years and drives all over hell from Quebec in a Ford Escort wagon, which my brother and I noticed had a rolled-up foam mattress in its stripped-out back.

He was one of the only guys in the competition who took the time to practice between events, intentionally nailing one of the 2-by-4 risers to the bottom of his underhand chop block 6 inches in from the end, rather than out flush. He then spiked the whole thing to the ground and got down on one knee in order to cut five or six wafers off the end with his bow saw. He didn't seem to mind the uncomfortable position or the fact that the last 2 inches of what must have been at least a $300 bowsaw blade kept stabbing into the gravelly soil. He was a big joker, despite knowing very little English, as well as being an extremely picky sawyer. In preparation for his heat in the one-man buck, Gaston made the competition's designated chain-saw lackey cut the billet back at least seven times before he was satisfied with the wood showing.

Tree Felling

The object of the felling contest is to drop your tree as quickly and accurately as possible using only an ax. Before the contest begins, each competitor places a pin in the ground at a specified distance from his trunk. The proper strategy is to study the angle and curvature of the tree, then mark out the felling notch on the fall side of the tree and the felling cut on the back side. At "go," competitors give a mighty uppercut to the bottom side of their felling notch, and then an equally deep shot from the top. A huge chip falls loose just ahead of the next uppercut, and so on, until a notch extending considerably more than halfway through the tree is cleaned out. Then it's quickly to the back side, where the single shot is the holy grail. The idea is to have notched the tree deeply enough that the fibers on the very outside of the back of the tree are under so much stress that a single deep whack in a spot directly opposite one's pin would be enough to topple the tree on the mark.

I didn't know it at the time, but the accuracy part is weighted heavily enough that fellers would actually stop and clean the chips out of the felling hinge, go around behind and sight things, and take single, deliberate swings with pauses in between. My tack was to rush feverishly to the tree and fly around it like a Tasmanian devil, a storm of chips and buzzing noises coming from the blur of my limbs. Perhaps a very creative person with

Chop chop. Tree-felling competitors go in five heats, so that there is one man spaced every five trees at a time. Competitors whittle their tree down to the diameter of the thinnest tree in the contest.

antiquated film technology could render this fantasy true, but what everyone else saw that day must have looked much more like a strong lad with no experience flailing furiously first at one side of the tree and then the other until (nearly 30 seconds after his fellow contestants) his tree fell in the very same county as the pin he had set for himself. I've learned a few tricks since then, and never been off by so much again.

Ax Throw

Competitors throw axes at a 36-inch-diameter target with a 4-inch bull's-eye; the ax must be thrown from behind a line 20 feet from the target. A bull's-eye nets five points, the next circle is worth four, and on down from there. An ax must weigh at least 2½ pounds and have a minimum handle length of 2 feet. A throwing ax is normally double bitted.

My own experience throwing hatchets tells me that you do not necessarily want to stand right at the line, but rather at the distance that allows the head of the ax to come around to the face of the target. For me, this happens every 12 paces. At 12, 24, and one day even 36 paces, I was able to repeat-release again and again, which brought the bit of the spinning hatchet smacking into various spots on a huge old white pine. This business about the 4-inch bull's-eye, though . . .

As is the case for other events, the nuances of the rules for the ax throw change from fair to fair. At one fair we attended, the highest-scoring ring touched by any part of one blade on the ax was the one recorded. If the ax over-rotated, and the point of the blade that would ideally be on the back side of the hatchet also stuck in the target, the throw was marked a zero. (Competitors would very carefully walk their axes back out of the wood, as the 6-inch-tall blades are dramatically flared and could well have passed through a higher-scoring ring before the wood closed behind them, possibly robbing the competitor of an inch or

1 That orange bull's-eye doesn't look much bigger in person; you need a sure aim to hit it.

2 Only one side of the double-bit ax is allowed to stick in the wood at once. This throw over-rotated a bit and was disqualified.

Watch your step. In birling, competitors roll smaller and smaller logs until one of them gets dunked.

so by exiting the wood lower or higher due to yanking.) Sometimes only three throws are allowed, and sometimes four, the score of the fourth throw to be counted only in the event of a tie. Once I was offered a practice throw, but this appears not to be the norm.

My friend Jake and I both competed in the ax throw, and he beat me with a score of six. I stuck all three throws but was allowing the ax slightly more than its ideal single flip, which resulted in two "double-pointers," as they were calling any throw resulting in both blades of the ax stuck in the target. These were misleading words, I was to find, as double-pointers are really worth zero points. Everyone was throwing with a two-handed, over-the-head motion. There was a lot of pantomiming and reaiming and squint-

ing and rocking, but when it came down to the release, all were trying to keep stiff wrists and to follow through with arms extended straight out in front of them.

Birling

This is the classic, comic discipline of trying to dump one's opponent in the water by running one way and the other on a log floating in the water. Logs are traditionally lathe-turned cedar ranging from 12 to 15 inches in diameter. Contestants roll progressively smaller logs until one person falls. Contests are usually determined by the best two out of three falls. The birler who remains on the log longer than his competitor in two runs out of three wins. Most small-town fairs just don't have the water for this event, much to my dismay.

Log Running

Contestants must sprint along a row of floating logs chained end to end from one dock to another and then back. The logs are not chained tightly to one another, and contestants without light enough feet, or who have mistimed their steps, find themselves trying to balance on something plunging underwater while they themselves are moving forward full steam. Most often people continue running even though they are heading sideways, and just dive into the drink. Sometimes, however, the right foot goes off the log to the left, for example, and the contestant comes down on the thing full blast with the rib cage, elbow, jaw, or hip.

Log Rolling

Log rolling is a two-person event. Each person has a stout peavey with a spike on the far end. (Peaveys are a bit tough to explain, so feel free to check the glossary on page 150 if necessary after reading the account.) Each roller pushes an end of the log as fast and hard as possible until it whacks into two posts set at the end of a roughly 60-foot course. The posts are set just a few inches closer together than the log is long, so your aim with this thing has to be pretty good. When it hits, both rollers leap over the now stationary log and shove it back where it came from, hitting two more posts at the other end. Sometimes this whole event takes place with the log on two rails, and the log cannot fall off the rails under penalty of disqualification. Read on, and you will encounter absolutely everything *not* to do in one of these contests.

When I signed up for log rolling, I assumed we were in for some birling, the log in the water and the spiked shoes we didn't have, and us in the water soon after. There was no water in sight, and I realized at once that these economical folk had meant just what they said, and we were to grab some loaner peaveys, or "cant dogs," and start rolling. The

Go fast, lumberjill. Contestants in log running must be swift-footed to get across the logs quickly, before they lose their balance and end up in the drink.

20-foot-long log was roughly 20 inches wide at one end and only 13 or so at the other. It was relatively free of bumps and curves, and the course was distinctly uphill on the first leg.

My friend Jake and I were the second team to go, and we felt pretty good about ourselves after watching the first hapless duo miss one of the pins at the far reach of their run. They quickly hooked their peaveys around the thick end and tugged parallel to the log to drag it back in line with the stakes. Lurching simultaneously to the side, they banged the log into the pin they had missed. Not to give it all away, but instead of strutting to the starting line, Jake and I should have been practicing that little dance a time or two. We quickly, incorrectly strategized that I should man the thick end, and Jake the narrow. In retrospect, we realized that this meant all of the aiming and steering was on him, and he was at that moment holding his first peavey. We dug in our dogs and waited for the call.

Like twin flashes of caffeinated lightning we cajoled our now-precious, now-despised log up the first leg of the race. To my joy we went very fast and hit the pins dead on. Having leapt the log as it was still rolling, we were turning and giving the first shove as it stopped at the stakes.

At this moment something went very wrong with our log, and I compounded things by spazzing out entirely. I was the one who laid out the surgical procedure for righting a

Roll with it. Bernard Peters and one of his clan get active with their peaveys in the log roll.

runaway log. I had told Jake that should the thick end get too far ahead, I would pin it momentarily in place with my peavey while he urged his end forward. That moment had come, for some reason, and it happened real fast. My competitive instinct would not let me slow the progress of the log at all, but instead I grew crazed with the desire to nurture our newfound downhill speed. I broke ranks and ran around back of Jake and began pushing furiously at the slender terminus, hoping that multiple shoves would bring it back parallel to the fat, juggernaut side. No such luck, and as I looked up I realized that we were a good 8 feet off course and closing on the nearest

Shimmy up. In the pole-climbing event, the competitor must scale a 100-foot pole in about 30 seconds.

we dragged the damned thing back abreast of the now-cobweb-covered stake and committed our final mistake of the ordeal to the background noise of the emcee saying, "This is their first time, folks. How 'bout a hand." Instead of simply tugging the log into the second stake to stop the clock, we hopped back onto its far side and gave it one final shove.

When the dust settled Jake and I sat comfortably in second-to-last place, behind at least two teams of burly women and ahead of one team of seasoned competitors with a combined age of more than 120 years.

Pole Climbing

Competitors race against the clock to climb and then descend a tall, limbed tree trunk. Large spikes ("spurs") mounted along the inside of each ankle, as well as a short length of rope looped from hand to hand around the pole, are the only forms of assistance the climbers have. A bell, placed at the top of the pole, must be struck before the descent. While descending, the climbers must set a spur at least once every 15 feet. Competitive times in the climb average around 30 seconds on a 100-foot-tall pole. Because of the difficulty of setting up one of these poles and the number of people injured, pole climbing is usually presented only at the biggest televised competitions. Even Fryeburg, the largest show east of the Mississippi, does not have a pole-climbing setup.

single pin fast. We stopped pushing, and as the log foundered in a really lonely way on the solo stake, we attempted to latch on to the fat, slightly rotted offending end.

Jake dug in first and tugged, but alone he was useless. As he repositioned himself I got a good grip and tugged frantically but without a partner. These thrashings pulled his peavey loose from its grip, and as he leaned in with me it tore loose. Then my grip faltered, and we both tried to reset simultaneously. Eventually

Methanol to the Madness

Frank

Chain saws are powerful and loud to begin with, but competitors in the hot saw competition have clearly decided that their chain saws need to be much bigger and produce a noise somewhere between the Rolling Stones being electrocuted in a Quonset hut and a cat in a cyclotron. These saws seem to have only a few requirements: They must start by means of a pull-cord, have only one cylinder (provenance unimportant), and cut wood like a son of a beech.

The ones I saw met all three requirements. One was made from an old, bored-out, chopped-down engine. One was a single cylinder from a large motorcycle engine, and it had the sole of an old boot wedged between the cigar-shaped muffler and the rest of the saw to cut down vibration. These things ran on all types of wacky fuel, but the one I was able to remember long enough to commit to paper was methanol with a 120-octane count and 6 percent nitromethane. I was warned that the stuff was incredibly flammable and unstable by a guy pouring the fuel back out of the saw, which had a dangerously hot muffler. I asked why it had to come back out, and why some of the fuel was leaking rapidly out the side of the saw away from the gas cap. His answer to the first half of the question made perfect sense, and his answer to the second half made me want to dive theatrically behind a truck inches ahead of a 50-foot fireball.

"We run mainly this methanol he-urr, ahnd it c'rodes thuh enjuhn to let it set in there. We hafta put gas back in and run it fer a minute t'clean her owt. Reason it's pourin' owt is I drilled a buncha howles ta let in mower ayer."

These fellas were from the Canadian border of Vermont and loggers by trade. Their accents were so thick, and endearing, and hysterical that I forgot that a man was telling me of a strategy wherein he *intentionally drilled holes through the top of his gas tank*. One might call it devotion.

Pulpwood Throw

The pulp throw is simply the throwing of a chunk of pine with the aid of a pulp hook. Contestants are allowed to execute any variety of lead-up they see fit, so long as their feet don't cross the line, the hook doesn't go flying, and the wood stays between two divergent lines heading out from the ends of the throwing line.

Some guys I observed shuffled up to the line sideways, loaded their weight and the log back, and cranked forward. At least two tried a more overhand approach, and for one giddy, dangerous moment a husky lad from Vermont was doing a brief walk-through of a discus-type spinning release movement. He was talked out of it. I tossed about 30 feet on the first go but didn't feel I was getting the force from my bottom hand and its pulp hook that I should have. I was afraid to sink the hook too deeply, as that would just cause the wood to flip very fast at release, and not arch out away at a 45-degree angle. Sinking the hook too lightly would result in some sort of premature tear-out and no distance either. Because the judges were marking the first dent in the ground, a cartwheeling approach was useless.

Pulp reality. I'm about to chuck a major hunk of pine in the pulpwood throw.

Hack job. This sawyering granny ("Grandmas can still cut it," her shirt says) chews up the wood during the single buck event.

One-Man Crosscut

As the name implies, this event allows only one competitor to run the saw. No weight or any device can be hung on the free end. The most difficult thing to overcome here is the buckling and bowing of these expensive saws. The majority of the cutting is done on the push stroke, as much more force can be put on the teeth this way. However, the idea is to put as long a stroke as possible into the cut, so the saw gets drawn out to its very last teeth. Brute strength and endurance are the main requisites for this one. I saw only two-man and Jack-and-Jill crosscuts at the events I entered, so to my mind I witnessed the trickier, more precisely choreographed aspects of sawyering anyway.

Single Buck

This event is similar to the one-man crosscut, with the only difference being the saw itself. In this case, the cutting tool is a bow saw rather than a crosscut saw. The saw has a bow-shaped frame, basically a long bar running parallel to the blade with the ends curved down to meet the blade stretched in between. Holes are drilled in the thin, bandlike blade, which hooks to both downturned ends of the frame. By folding a lever on the end of the saw upward, the competitor can stretch the blade incredibly tightly in its frame. When it is locked in like this, the thin, normally flexible blade feels like an iron rod when you tap it or try to twist it out of shape. The frame is relatively cheap, but the blades are expensive; they can run $300 to $500.

Sawing one off. Mike Slingerland makes his way through the log during the one-man crosscut event.

Stroke! Stroke! Sawdust flies while Dave Jewett and J.P. Mercier get down to business in the two-man crosscut competition.

Two-Man Crosscut

See "One-Man Crosscut," and add another person. In each of the sawing events contestants can have a helper who sprays the saw with a lubricant and gently pushes little wedges into the top side of the cut to keep the saw from binding. Usually, contestants must make two vertical cuts all the way through the wood. Each cut through a 10 by 10 can be done in four strokes by an experienced team. The fastest time I saw at one fair was turned in by a husband-and-wife team. The second fastest time at the fair was turned in by another husband-and-wife team. The third-place time was turned in by one of those husbands and his male partner, a hulking specimen of typical woodsmanship, but no match in technique for some of the ladies.

The trick in this competition, aside from having the best saw (over two grand), is to weigh how much downward pressure can be put on the blade before it stalls. If the person pushing exerts more lateral pressure than the person pulling, then the pushing side of the blade will bow and pinch in the wood. This is death to a competitive time. The other area where time can be gained or lost is in the transition from the first cut to the second. Members of a team who really know one another will know exactly when in the third or fourth stroke the wood will be severed and will swing directly into the next pass through the wood while moving the blade back to the top of the wood. The visual effect is one-half of a full-stroke sequence made in the air, traveling upward rather than down, and then right back into the wood in the same sequence that started the first cut. When this is done expertly, two discs can be cut from a log faster than I can do it with a chain saw.

Jack-and-Jill Crosscut

Same as the two-man, but one of the men isn't. I have seen this event a number of times, and these women are incredible powerhouses.

Stock Saw

In most competitions, this is a three-cut event (down, up, down) with a saw that has not been modified in any way. Contestants must start with their hands on the log to be cut, with the saw at their feet. At the signal, they drop their hands to the saw, fire it on the first pull (or they're doomed), and cut three discs from the end of a log ranging from 8 to 18 inches. Timing stops when the last disc is fully severed.

I have sensed some tension around the edges of this subject, with big strong purists complaining that there are too many chain-saw events, which ends up weighting the overall scoring away from "hand events." Loggers and gearheads tend to like the chain-saw events, and there are two representative disciplines in both the Stihl Timbersports Series and the Great Outdoor Games. Being a purist at heart, and old-timey when I can, I would ordinarily have been against the introduction of chain saws. This day was far from ordinary for me though, and I saw a stock chain-saw contest as a level playing field for someone as underequipped as I was. Hah.

Before the competition began, contestants were told to do whatever they wished to warm up the saw and then to turn it off, set

Girl power. Some of the best two-person crosscut teams I watched were Jack-and-Jill.

Rev it up. In the stock saw event, 11 seconds is a competitive time to complete the three necessary cuts — down, up, then down again — on a 16-inch log.

New Ax Shopping

After my first competition, I was still smarting from being advised to "go bury that ax in the woods." I wondered at the time whether it was due to the splice in the handle because of the removal of 6 inches of length or the dings in the blade that made it look like a toothless smile. Either way, I was determined to get my hands on a real chopper.

I got in touch with a man in Wisconsin who imports, sharpens, and "hangs" Australian and Kiwi ax heads (to "hang," remember, means to fit a handle to). He was a nice guy, and head of the United States Axemen's Association to boot. I had forgotten that I had entered a very small, tight community and was floored when he mailed a $200 ax to me sight unseen, check unwritten. I kept telling him on the phone that it would go out at the end of the week, and he told me he didn't care and would send it anyway. In retrospect, this is really not the bunch of people you want angry with you, and I don't imagine they get ripped off too frequently.

The ax came in a long, thin cardboard box, which contained a warning label that had to be bypassed before getting to the good stuff. As I was savoring this moment anyway, my puritan roots compelled me to delay my reward just a bit more and read the thing. I was informed that I was solely responsible from the moment I hit my first piece of wood, and to make sure that wood was neither frozen nor mud encrusted. I was also warned that this was merely a practice ax, and not to be trusted in matters of precision. I hauled the thing out and immediately forgot all of the caveats. It was beautiful. Shiny as chrome, smelling of WD-40, flared impossibly wide along the blade with an angular, rough-hewn oak handle and a shiny little pin driven through the head at the top. This thin little rod was the only thing about it that bespoke safety of any kind.

Looking at this ax suddenly gave me a powerful pang of homesickness, not for a house or friend or relative, but for one decent piece of white pine. I was keenly aware of standing in a brick building on a tar street in a cement neighborhood. I wasn't within an hour of something I could cut safely, and it was more than 3 hours to something legal. I walked around the apartment cutting strings, halving paper, shaving stretches of my arms, and even at one point easily slicing up the last 4 inches of a hard salami. In case you had ever wondered, WD-40 goes just as well with salami as you would expect, but I didn't care. I had honestly not gotten so excited about a tool since receiving a chain saw for college graduation.

it near the wood, and put both hands on top of the pine to be cut. After a "one, two, three, go!" hands dropped to find both handle and pull-cord. As the left hand raised the saw the right hand jerked the starter once and shot directly to the throttle; instantly opened all the way up, the saw slammed down on the wood harder than anyone would normally treat a saw. The three cuts were made, and the saw extinguished. Winning times were around 6 seconds.

I have no idea now why I thought this was a level playing field, except for the fact that I have run saws for hundreds and hundreds of hours. I was due to go fourth, and I watched those before me very carefully. Most guys were doing a little something to keep the handle away from the body of the saw, but I didn't notice it at first. Before raising their hands to the billet, they would grab a little handful of sawdust with the left hand and toss it against the side of the saw while fiddling with the starter cord with the right hand. I thought it was just a way to dry sweat while nervously fiddling with the starter. Not so. As the contestants tipped the pull start to the side they were tossing the sawdust into its little socket, propping it out from the casing of the saw. Most of these handles are designed to be out of the way after the saw has been started, and this streamlining saves precious fractions on the clock in a contest like this.

When it was my turn, I did the same thing and hoped it would counteract the fact that I had never started a saw so recklessly in my life. I got what I thought to be a pretty good jump, and after a smooth start and a slight reset before the first cut, I pushed and pulled that Dolmar (a brand no one knows anything about) right to the point of bogging down on three consecutive cuts to the safe side of the line. I finished in 7.5 seconds. To me, this is a lifetime in a race whose winning time was 6 seconds.

Hot Saw

This is the same event as described for the stock saw, but with a heavily modified, incredibly powerful, expensive saw. Three full cuts

Not your grandpa's muffler. These saws have massive mufflers to attain the right exhaust backpressure, which is necessary in a high-rpm, two-stroke engine to help each piston reload.

through a 14-inch round of yellow poplar in 4 seconds is what we're dealing with here. Not your daddy's saw. Unless your dad is one of these guys.

These things are barely recognizable as chain saws; often made from motorcycle or Jet Ski engines cut in half (the saw must be only one cylinder), they run on methanol or some other incredibly combustible fuel derivative and make an incredible racket. One of these monsters can weigh up to 70 pounds, and it must be yanked from the ground and passed through a piece of wood three times, down-up-down, in under 4 seconds for an even remotely successful run. The bars of the saws are sometimes over 6 inches tall, and the reason is frightening. Even when stretched tightly, these chains are traveling so fast that the centripetal forces acting on them pull them away from the bar after they have passed the engine and bar-tip sprockets.

The obvious solution? Go back to a regular chain saw, you say? Hell no! Simply order up an elliptical bar from Ontario, Canada, one that more closely matches the path a chain wants to take at such ridiculous speeds. Think of these modified bars and chains as racetracks and the cars that circle them; the faster they go, the more forgiving the turns have to be to keep them on the track.

Hot stuff. Competitors in the hot saw event make three cuts with the saw in less than 4 seconds.

Though I personally witnessed only four hot saw competitions, I saw two accidents. Before I knew this particular event was so dangerous, I noticed the portable metal screens officials haul solemnly out onto the infield to protect the onlookers. Each of these screens is a tall set of panels with hinges at the top and chains keeping them from folding all the way out, much like a stepladder; it is designed to keep errant and destroyed chains and engine parts from flinging off into the innocent world at large. I thought this a bit excessive at first, but lo and behold, the second time I saw these woodland cowboys strolling out to the pitch in their chaps and steel toes, a man's saw failed him. He got down through his first cut all right, but he seemed to lose his balance some on the way back up. He didn't regain a steady stance but headed down hard into his third cut. I found out later that he had hit the wood at a funny angle, and at that moment the chain on his saw had started out of its track. He was halfway down the last cut when one of his legs flew back suddenly, and the cut portion of the billet flew violently into the air just over his right shoulder. I knew something was wrong before he turned, grinning to his friends with a jarring cluster of fluffy and snarled Kevlar fibers jutting from his left thigh.

"Went in a little crooked, I guess," was all he could say of the now-inert chain hanging at a decidedly inappropriate angle from the top of his engine housing. It had flown loose, flung the partially cut disc of wood into the air, and then whipped him mightily across the thigh before stopping. The same thing happened to another competitor that day. They must have lost more money on the chaps they destroyed than they stood to win in the contest.

The end

Adz: This is an old-style ax with the blade mounted perpendicularly to the handle, as on a hoe. It was used for hewing beams to square angles before mechanized saws were in use.

Ax: An ax is the woodsman's proto-tool. Most of colonial and frontier New England and, for that matter, the Pacific Northwest were cleared with this simple, versatile tool. The modern ax doesn't do much more than sit in most people's garages, but there is a devoted, highly skilled subculture of competitive lumberjacks who have kept alive man's vital relationship with this tool.

An ax is for chopping; a maul is for splitting (see *Maul*). The traditional ax has a much thinner, taller blade than a maul, as well as a recurved handle. The maul has a blunter blade that is not so tall. The head of a maul weighs two to three times as much as an ax head. You will know the difference because a maul simply will not cut a piece of wood perpendicular to the grain, while an ax will stick repeatedly in a piece of wood going with the grain, rather than splitting it in two as a maul will. An ax handle has an aggressively ovoid shape when viewed in cross section, whereas a maul has a straight handle that is circular or slightly ovoid in cross section.

Bar: This is the rigid, vertical metal bar that is bolted to the side of a chain-saw engine and juts forward. It has a couple of very simple features. A groove in the edge of the bar keeps the teeth that protrude from the bottom or inside of the chain running in a perfectly straight line. The bar has a sprocket at the end, around which the chain runs; it must be oiled and catch free in order for the chain to run fast and smooth. The sprocket is susceptible to pinching in a falling tree or improperly cut horizontal wood. If the metal housing holding the sprocket is pinched too hard, it will retain its new shape and slow the sprocket. This in turn will slow the chain and add a lot of heat to the situation.

Bar and chain oil: Chain saws require this oil, which is stored and deployed separately from the gasoline. It feeds down onto the sprocket at the engine and is drawn out along the top of the bar to the sprocket at the end of the bar.

Billet: This is simply a term for a short, thick length of wood, possibly to be carved or lathe-turned into a finer, more specific product.

Bolt: A bolt of wood is a length that has not been machined; a round of wood.

Bow saw: The modern bow saw is probably the suburban homeowner's answer to the chain saw, but only for dealing with fallen branches and taking down the occasional limb. It is far cheaper and easier to maintain than a chain saw, and with practice it is almost as fast through any log or branch under 10 inches in diameter. The bow saw is so named because it resembles a bow of the bow-and-arrow variety, as well as a bow used for playing fiddle. The principle here is the same. Instead of relying on the stiffness of a metal blade, as in a traditional handsaw, the bow saw relies on the tensile strength of a thin ribbon of a blade stretched very tightly between the arms of a bow. Older models have a stiff bar parallel to the blade, and on the other side of that a length of rope that can be twisted and tightened, thereby stretching the blade even more tightly. The tighter the blade, the more it resembles a perfectly rigid blade and the more easily it flies through softwoods like pine and poplar.

Bow saws have what is referred to as a very aggressive "rake" or "set" to their teeth. This means that if you were to sight along the blade, you would actually see that each tooth is bent outward in the opposite direction as the previous tooth. What this does is effectively clear the path for the blade as it goes, so that it doesn't get stuck. It also means that the blade takes big gouges of material with each stroke. As my closest college friend once found, this leads very quickly to stitches when dragged across the thumb.

Btu: This is the acronym for British thermal unit; 1 Btu is a unit of energy equivalent to the work done by 1,000 watts working for 1 hour.

Buck up: To buck up wood is to cut it down to stove-length pieces.

Chain: A chain saw's chain is much like a bicycle chain, though thinner and stiffer in side-to-side movement. It has three components: cutting teeth, risers, and two-dimensional teeth protruding from the cutting teeth. The cutting teeth are staggered: left-side cutter, right-side cutter, and so on. Each riser, which is a little bump just forward of each cutting tooth, keeps that tooth from biting too deeply, and thereby bogging down. The risers need to be filed down at the same rate as the cutting teeth, or the blade will cut more and more slowly. Each cutting tooth has a flat, two-dimensional tooth jutting downward from it. These are the teeth that are driven by the sprocket protruding from the engine. They slide through the groove in the bar and roll over the sprocket at the bar's end.

Chain saw: Every woodsman's most indispensable tool, the chain saw revolutionized the logging industry. The small, lightweight (nowadays) saw pioneered by Andreas Stihl will run fast at any angle and cut wood for years and years if properly maintained. A wonderful and productive tool when used properly, the chain saw is extremely dangerous and harmful if mistreated or used casually.

Chain tensioner: This is a screw that acts as a small worm gear, which when tightened or loosened moves the bar toward or away from the saw to adjust the tension on the chain.

Chaps: These leggings made of Prolar or some similar material will bind up the chain instantly if touched when the chain saw is running. They should be able to turn a possible amputation into a wicked bruise.

Cribbing: This column of cordwood is formed by cross-hatching the pieces of wood at the ends of a freestanding pile; it takes the spreading force of all the parallel-stacked pieces in between.

Dogs: These sharp, upward-facing teeth mounted where the bar meets the chain saw are used for leverage and stability. They can be jammed lightly into wood while the bar is pointing upward and then used as a pivot point while the handle is lifted, driving the bar down through the wood without undue pressure on the nontrigger hand. Digging in the dogs often provides a welcome rest to the chain-saw wielder.

Eye: For our purposes, the eye of an ax or maul is the ovoid, rather eye-shaped hole running through the head, into which the handle is fitted. This process is called "hanging the head."

Felling wedge: This refers to a plastic wedge, not unlike a doorstop and about 8 inches long and 8 inches wide. It is meant to be expendable, as the blade of the chain saw must often come into contact with the leading edge of the wedge. Most of our wedges have been eaten away so far back that the chewed-up edge is in danger of meeting the mushroomed edge. (Something that has been pounded repeatedly with a hammer or maul and has expanded and split and rolled over is said to be "mushroomed." Think of the typical cartoon tent stake.)

Fireplace insert: This is basically a stove that's installed in a recessed position, inside an existing fireplace. Inserts are much more efficient than traditional fireplaces, but slightly less efficient and slightly dirtier than stoves featuring the same size firebox. The advantage is that they take up less space. If you don't want the stove out in the room and don't mind the noise of the requisite blowers (to get the heat out of the alcove and into the room), then one of these might be worth looking into.

Hang up: To hang up a tree means to get it caught in a stand of trees when it's being felled. This is easier to do than you might think, as the tree really does not develop a lot of momentum until it is more than 10 to 15 degrees from vertical, leaving a tree with many branches plenty of opportunity to get hung up.

Hardwood: This is the opposite of pulpwood. Pulpwoods are most often coniferous and hardwoods are deciduous. Prime examples of hardwoods are ash, maple, oak, and hickory. Pulpwoods, or softwoods, are white pine, spruce, hemlock, red pine, Douglas fir, and hemlock. In general, hardwoods are better for heating.

Hatchet: The average hatchet looks like a miniature ax, though most do not have the recurved handle of the traditional ax. To be useful for lopping small limbs from trees or splitting kindling, a hatchet must be kept very sharp. A hatchet has limited use in cordwood procurement; I have used one much more while camping than during a lifetime of firewood work. However, there is no substitute for a good hatchet in one area of all this work, and that is in making kindling. This was actually the first activity I was ever allowed to do with a sharp tool.

I learned when I was very little to lightly strike the top of a piece of maple, or better yet ash, with nice straight, unknotted grain. When the hatchet stuck in such a way as to separate a small portion of the wood from the rest, I drove it down through with a 3-pound hammer. I got so good at this over the years that I could fill a kindling box almost without touching any of the wood with my hands. A light swing would stick the hatchet in the right spot and the hammer would drive it through each time until these two tools were acting

as delicate hands would, quickly steadying or rotating a piece of wood while paring it down into kindling.

Hydraulic splitter: An extremely powerful hydraulic piston with a blade mounted on it, this simple machine can split any wood you throw at it and is relatively reasonable to rent.

Limb: As a verb, to limb a tree is actually to *de*-limb it. Limbing comes after felling and before bucking up.

Maul: To the uninitiated, a maul is just a big, heavy, dull ax. The best modern ones are of one-piece construction, featuring a heavy metal tube of a handle welded into a 10-pound head with a rugged wedge for a blade. This crude tool, when wielded by someone of experience against wood that is willing (not too knotty), can be even faster than a hydraulic splitting machine. A maul can also be used for driving splitting wedges through "tough customers" and for forcing a felling wedges into felling cut on a tree that may not want to go the way you desire. The maul is far superior than an ax for splitting wood. Remember, an ax is for chopping, and a maul is for splitting. Also see *Ax*.

Peavey: This tool is devoted to leverage and safe bucking of logs. It consists of a very stout handle around 40 inches long that meets the socket of a heavy spike and fulcrum. Attached to the spike is what appears to be half of a pair of ice tongs. The wielder uses the curved hook to latch onto a log when the hook is perpendicular to it and, by forcing the handle downward, rolls the log back onto the fulcrum on the bottom of the peavey. The log rests there, a few inches off the ground, while the woodsman bucks it up. By doing this continually down the length of a felled tree, the peavey wielder can keep cutting wood up in the air, rather than having to cut three-quarters through a log in five places and then roll it by hand to finish each cut.

Peeling: A splitting technique for larger pieces of wood, peeling consists of taking small pieces from around the edges of a bolt (a short round section of a log) until the main chunk can be attacked realistically.

Poll: The poll is the blunt side of an ax or maul head, opposite the blade. The poll can be used for hammering wedges if needed but basically exists to add more heft to your swing (which we all need).

Pulp hook: A specialized but occasionally very useful device, this is a large, strong hook mounted on what looks like a slightly thinner shovel handle, so that the hook is in the position of an extended finger, right in line with the hand. The hook is whacked into the end grain of any billet of wood so that it can be more easily hoisted by one person. And it makes a really good scary Halloween prop for use on those who have never seen one.

Pulpwood: See *Hardwood*.

Sap spout: This is an old tin or aluminum spout tapped into a predrilled hole in a sugar maple tree to drip sap into a bucket that hangs from the spout.

Sapwood: The sapwood in any tree is the layer of wood beginning just inside the bark. In full-grown specimens, it's just a few inches wide.

Soot: This is a catchall term for fine black particles, mostly carbon, deposited in chimneys after the incomplete combustion of fuels such as coal, oil, and wood.

Spark plug: As in any internal combustion engine, the chain saw has a spark plug for its one cylinder. The plug supplies the ignition for the gasoline.

Splitting wedge: Similar to the felling wedge in name only, this is a 3- to 5-pound iron wedge about 2½ inches wide and 2 inches thick, with a rounded poll for hammering with a sledge or maul. Using a splitting wedge is tantamount to saying that you absolutely must have that particular piece in your stove, or you are blighted with firewood so consistently bad that you should consider natural gas. Splitting wedges are slow and cumbersome to use and tend to get stuck in anything but relatively clear wood, which should preclude the use of one anyway. I am not a fan, but if you are the type of perfectionist who must split each piece you have bucked up and not consecrate anything unwillingly to the fireplace, then you might as well have one kicking around.

A word of warning: If a splitting wedge has become too mushroomed (see *Felling wedge*) or mangled at the impact end, it will not only resist passage through the wood, but may well fire small pieces of metal at you when struck. This is no joke. I was once cut very cleanly on the cheek by a fragment of metal leaving the wedge at such speed that I had no time to react.

Sprocket: The toothed wheel at the end of the bar is a sprocket. Little ball bearings make it spin.

Two-stroke engine: The engines of chain saws, lawn mowers, and older motorcycles are two-stroke engines. They run faster and dirtier than auto engines because fuel is combusted twice as often as in four-stroke engines. The four-stroke engine allows each piston to pump one time in the cylinder without any fuel being injected. In a two-stroke engine, fuel explodes in the cylinder each time the piston travels down, allowing for more power and more exhaust.

Btu Values by Species

If this has all been too much fun and too few numbers and charts and such, here is a table of wood species arranged alphabetically, with their respective weights and Btus per cord. Look through it when you have determined what you have on your property, and you'll be able to make a more informed decision about what to burn, as well as which kinds of trees to promote on your woodlot.

Wood Species	Weight (lbs/cord)	Million Btus/cord	Wood Species	Weight (lbs/cord)	Million Btus/cord
Alder	2,708	17.6	Fir, Balsam	2,236	14.3
Apple	4,140	26.5	Fir, Douglas	3,196	20.6
Ash, Black	2,992	19.1	Hackberry	3,247	20.8
Ash, White	3,689	23.6	Hemlock	2,482	15.9
Aspen	2,295	14.7	Hickory	4,327	27.7
Basswood	2,108	13.5	Hornbeam, Eastern	4,267	27.3
Beech, Blue	3,890	26.8	Locust, Black	3,890	26.8
Beech, High	3,757	24.0	Maple, Red	2,924	18.7
Birch, Black	3,890	26.8	Maple, Sugar	3,757	24.0
Birch, Gray	3,179	20.3	Oak, Red	3,757	24.0
Birch, Paper	3,179	20.3	Oak, White	4,012	25.7
Birch, White	3,179	20.3	Pine, Jack	2,669	17.1
Birch, Yellow	3,689	23.6	Pine, Norway	2,669	17.1
Box elder	2,797	17.9	Pine, Pitch	2,669	17.1
Butternut	2,100	14.5	Pine, Ponderosa	2,380	15.2
Cedar, White	1,913	12.2	Pine, Western	2,236	14.3
Cherry	3,120	20	Spruce	2,100	14.5
Cherry, Black	2,880	19.9	Spruce, Black	2,482	15.9
Cottonwood	2,108	13.5	Tamarack (Larch)	3,247	20.8
Elm, American	3,052	19.5	Willow	2,100	14.5
Elm, Oven	3,052	19.5			
Elm, White	3,052	19.5			

How Much to Expect (Volume in Cords)

The table below will allow you to accurately estimate what part of a cord you should get from any given tree, and thereby to know when you've reached your target for the year, long before you start splitting and stacking the wood.

Total Tree Height

Diameter (at breast height)	20'	30'	40'	50'	60'	70'	80'	90'	100'
4"	0.005	0.007	0.010	0.012	0.015				
5"	0.010	0.013	0.020	0.024	0.029	0.032			
6"	0.016	0.022	0.030	0.037	0.045	0.050			
7"	0.023	0.032	0.043	0.054	0.065	0.078	0.083		
8"		0.043	0.059	0.074	0.090	0.100	0.120	0.140	
9"		0.056	0.076	0.095	0.120	0.140	0.160	0.180	
10"		0.070	0.095	0.120	0.140	0.160	0.200	0.220	0.250
11"			0.120	0.150	0.170	0.210	0.240	0.270	0.300
12"			0.140	0.180	0.200	0.250	0.290	0.310	0.360
13"			0.150	0.210	0.240	0.300	0.340	0.390	0.430
14"			0.180	0.230	0.290	0.340	0.400	0.450	0.500
15"			0.230	0.290	0.340	0.400	0.460	0.520	0.580
16"			0.260	0.330	0.390	0.460	0.530	0.600	0.670
17"			0.280	0.370	0.450	0.530	0.600	0.680	0.760
18"			0.330	0.420	0.500	0.590	0.680	0.770	0.860
19"			0.370	0.470	0.560	0.660	0.760	0.860	0.960
20"			0.410	0.520	0.630	0.740	0.850	0.960	1.070
21"				0.580	0.700	0.820	0.940	1.070	1.190
22"				0.640	0.770	0.910	1.040	1.180	1.310
23"				0.700	0.850	1.000	1.150	1.290	1.440
24"				0.760	0.930	1.100	1.260	1.420	1.580
25"				0.830	1.010	1.180	1.370	1.540	1.720
26"				0.900	1.100	1.270	1.470	1.650	1.850
27"				0.970	1.180	1.380	1.590	1.800	2.000
28"				1.040	1.270	1.490	1.710	1.930	2.150
29"				1.130	1.370	1.600	1.850	2.080	2.320
30"				1.210	1.470	1.720	1.980	2.240	2.490

Recommended Reading

Common Sense Forestry
by Hans Morsbach
Chelsea Green, 2002

The New Woodburner's Handbook
by Stephen Bushway
Storey Publishing, 1992

Reading the Forested Landscape
by Tom Wessels
Countryman Press, 2005

Storey's Basic Country Skills: A Practical Guide to Self-Reliance
by John and Martha Storey
Storey Publishing, 1999

The Woodlot Management Handbook
by Stewart Hilts and Peter Mitchell
Firefly Books, 1999

*Working with Your Woodland:
A Landowner's Guide*
by Mollie Beattie, Charles Thomson,
and Lynn Levine
University Press of New England, 1993

Choosing the Right Saw

Throughout the pages of this book, we've weighed in on the Husky/Stihl debate. You should know, though, that there *are* other brands of chain saws readily available at home improvement and building supply stores everywhere. They include: Craftsman, Homelite, Jonsered, Makita, McCulloch, Poulan, Remington, and Shindaiwa, among others.

Within each brand you'll find a number of models with a variety of engine sizes, bar lengths, and prices. Keep in mind that buying a chain saw is not like buying a set of golf clubs or a pair of skis; just because you're taller or manlier than the average Joe doesn't mean you should buy the biggest saw with the longest bar you can find. These mammoth saws are meant to be used by the kind of professional loggers who make their living despoiling stands of 800-year-old redwoods, not by Joe Homeowner who wants to cut down a few birch saplings. Take a gander at the table opposite and carefully consider how you'll be using your saw (and how often) before you lay out the cash.

A Quick-Reference Guide to Chain Saw Features and Appropriate Use

	Intended use	Engine size	Horsepower (hp)	Saw weight	Bar length	Price
Lightweight Lumberjacking	occasional homeowner use cutting down saplings and pruning damaged branches limbing felled trees	2–2.5 cubic inches	2–2.3 hp	7–8 pounds	12–14 inches	$
Backyard Lumberjacking	frequent homeowner use felling trees up to 24 inches in diameter limbing and bucking up felled trees	2.7–4.5 cubic inches	3.4–5.4 hp	10.5–14.5 pounds	15–20 inches	$$
Professional Lumberjacking	frequent professional use felling trees larger than 24 inches in diameter	5.2–7.3 cubic inches	6.3–8.4 hp	15–23 pounds	20–36 inches	$$$

acknowledgments

Thanks to Bacon's Power Equipment for two clean chain saws and a load of other tools; the Stevens family for advice and a loaner ax; Rich Jordan for putting my feet in the right place; Mark Gould for the shoes that fit; and Bernard Peters for showing me "it weren't for the money, just to see who we could beat." Thanks to Ma Jennings, the Cinder Block, and young Bocephus for "my first bucksaw." Adam and Charlie, Carleen and Deb, Kent and Vicky, and anyone else who had to wrangle us — thanks to you for showing patience beyond all need. — *F.P.*

Thanks to Dorsey, Harry Guyette, Fran Henry, and Bud of Bud's. — *S.P.*

Special thanks to Marc Volk, Hearthlink International (www.hearthlink.com), Hearthstone Stoves (www.hearthstonestoves.com), Bacon's Equipment (www.baconsequipment.com), CFM Corporation (www.vermontcastings.com), and Jøtul, USA (www.jotul.us). — *eds.*

Photography Credits

Interior photographs by Adam Mastoon, except for the following:
© Loetscher Chlaus/Alamy: 83 top left
© Nick Haslam/Alamy: 83 top right
© Imagebroker/Alamy: 83 bottom left
© David Lyons/Alamy: 83 bottom right
© Steve Bowman: 122, 127, 132, 135, 136, 138, 139 bottom, 141 bottom, 142, 143 bottom, 145, 146
Courtesy of CFM Corporation: 99 bottom right
© Lynne & Marvin Carlton/2C imagery: 1 bottom
© Gabriel Cooney: 65 bottom, 82
© Royalty-free/Corbis: 95
Courtesy of Dagan Industries: 101
Courtesy of Lincoln Fish: 56
© Photodisc/Getty Images: 39 top, 91, 92 bottom, 117 bottom
© Photographer's Choice/Getty Images: 1 top
Courtesy of Hearthlink, International: 99 top left and bottom left
© Fran Henry: 3 right, 71, 80 top
Courtesy of Jøtul, USA: 99 top right
Kent Lew: v

Library of Congress, Prints and Photographs Division: (LC-USF34-030684-D) 13, (LC-USZ62-67624) 17 top, (clockwise from top left: LC-USF34-073465-D, LC-USF34-030036-E, LC-USF34-073563-E, LC-USF34-073437-D, LC-USF34-073460-D, LC-USF34-073447-D) 63, (LC-USZ62-69215) 98, (LC-USF34-073541-E) 125 top, (LC-USF33-013187-M2) 125 bottom
© Tex McLeod: 88
© Cory E. Mescon: 123 top, 124
© Katie Naka: xiv, 140, 147
Courtesy of Parry Sound Public Library: 126
Carleen Madigan Perkins: 9, 14 bottom right, 96
© Stephen Philbrick: 65 top, 91 top, 107 top
Dan Reynolds: 109
Ilona Sherratt: 14 all except bottom row right, 15, 81, 102 right, 103
Jonathan Sherrill, courtesy of the Forbes Library, Northampton, MA: 23
© Meg Simone: 128-131, 133, 137, 141 top, 143 top
Courtesy of Tom Wessels: 6
Vicky Vaughn: 102 left